The Special Relationship - A modern American woman's **guide** to finding love with a British man

Frederica Noble

Clink Street

Published by Clink Street Publishing 2021

Copyright © 2021

First edition.

ISBN:
978-1-913962-60-9 - paperback
978-1-913962-61-6 - ebook

I wrote this book in loving memory of my parents, Mai Dee and Frederick Hendricks. They taught me to love and how to look for the goodness in people regardless of race, creed, sexual orientation or ethnicity. They showed me what it meant to be of service to others and the importance of giving back to society. Most importantly, they empowered me, supported my ideas, gave me hope and helped me become the woman I am today.

Preface

Why do American women fall in love with English men? What is it about the English man that beguiles us? Is it the accent? Or the uniquely British dry wit and humour? Is it our romantic sensibility or fascination with royalty? Whatever the attraction, our history with men from across the Atlantic is well established. In the 19th century, American titans of power such as Willie Vanderbilt, used their money to arrange for their daughters to marry into British aristocracy for an increase in social status and a title. Typically, these American heiress brides came with a substantial dowry, which provided their soon-to-be husbands with a much-needed influx of cash. Vanderbilt's daughter, Consuelo, married Sunny, the Duke of Marlborough. Her millions helped him save his family pile, Blenheim Palace. A fictional account of this type of marriage was depicted in the popular television series *Downton Abbey*. The American, Jennie Jerome, was the daughter of a New York real estate magnate who married Lord Randolph Churchill. Her son Winston became one of the most famous and respected British Prime Ministers of the 20th century. Diana, Princess of Wales was the great-granddaughter of the American socialite Frances Ellen Work. Today, there are many successful Anglo-American pairings. Now, though, our fathers aren't marrying us off to some British aristocrat in order to gain a title. Modern American women are choosing their own Mr. Darcy, or in the case of Meghan Markle, a prince.

What makes the modern American woman different from her 20th century counterpart is that she typically has her own career, her own money, her own voice and can make up her own mind. She doesn't care about titles or where he went to school. Sure, it's nice if his family is landed gentry or you become a "Lady" instead of remaining a spinster, but in the big scheme of things it should come down to love and compatibility.

I love *James Bond, Elgar, Jamie Oliver, Queen, David Beckham, Othello, George Michael, Idris Elba* and the movies *Love Actually and The Crying Game.* My love for tea and Shakespeare was developed during my four years at Vassar, but did those "loves" mean I was ready to date an Englishman? No, of course not, but it was a good start. I had always wanted to live abroad. I didn't know exactly where I wanted to live or what I was going to do. The only pre-requisite was that I had to relocate to a country where English was spoken as the primary language in the workplace. Fate conspired with destiny and moving abroad became more of a reality than I ever imagined, as I fell in love with a man from "across the pond". Richard had been sent to America for one year. However, he was called back to England early, after just four months in Los Angeles. We tried to maintain a long-distance relationship but taking the 11.5-hour trip from LA to London became expensive and unduly stressful for both of us. Finally, after six months, we decided I should "hitch my wagon" to a British Airways 777 and set up residence in England if we wanted our relationship to work. I applied for a part-time university position, was shortlisted and was invited to interview on campus. My interview just happened to coincide with a visit to Richard I had already planned. I interviewed on Wednesday and was offered the job on Friday. I accepted the position, and my fate was sealed. There was so much to do before my move—say good-bye to family and friends, resign from my job at Loyola Marymount, terminate my apartment lease, sell my beloved car etc. It was April, and my appointment was to begin in August.

How did I prepare for the cross-continental move? I read Bill Bryson's *Notes from a Small Island.* I ate breakfast at *John O'Groats* on Pico Boulevard, gathered all my *Lands' End* clothing, held a garage sale and took my plants to Nashville to grow and thrive at my parents. I mistakenly thought relocating to England couldn't be that different from moving across the United States. I had traversed the States several times for school and work, so how hard would an intercontinental move be? Plus, I had been to the UK on holiday (as the English say) many times; I believed I was ready. How difficult could it be? I was in love and living my dream! Well, truth be told, I was underprepared and overwhelmed. The fact that I had a job and an English boyfriend did not make my move or adjustment to Great Britain easier. Furthermore, I was naïve to think that my speaking English would make the transition straightforward. So, if you are thinking about dating (or marrying) an Englishman and heading off to England, let me give you a few tips and offer some advice before you do. I wish I had the book you are about to read to better understand the man I fell in love with and to help me acclimatize to his country, his people, and English culture. It would have made my adjustment time shorter and less stressful. Moreover, I would have fallen in love with my second home country so much sooner. It would be impossible for me to cover all the glorious sites, vibrant culture and rich history that makes Great Britain great, and I apologize now for leaving out a lot more than I have included. I have, however, provided the reader with personal antidotes, quick tips, interesting facts and practical advice. The book is filled with everyday information needed to help you understand your Englishman a little better.

Wishing you all the best in love and life!
Frederica

Contents

CHAPTER 1

How Technology and a Map can Help Your First Date go well

I feel so fortunate to live and love in these modern times. Although, I am old enough to have used a rotary telephone and a typewriter, I can't remember the last time I used either to call someone or write a love letter. Technology has changed the way we meet, date, socially interact and communicate with people. We are now able to locate almost anyone, anywhere, at any time thanks to the Internet, social media and access to a smartphone. It is easier now to connect and keep in touch, even over long distances. The days of writing an advert and placing it in the personal classified section of your city's local magazine or newspaper don't exist anymore. There are many traditional ways today's modern woman can meet the man of her dreams (e.g., work, church, school, travelling). However, she also has access to relationship sites and dating apps, which are common features of our everyday life now. Of course, the old-fashioned way of being introduced to someone by a family member or a mutual friend also still works. No matter how you come to meet your Englishman, use technology to learn more about him. Look at his *Facebook* or *LinkedIn* page. Does he have a social media presence? Does he use *Twitter*, *TikTok* or *Instagram*? Take some time to investigate his digital footprint. If he doesn't have one, what does that tell you? Could it be that he is an international man of mystery and works for MI6? Probably not, but make this a fun endeavour – you could uncover some useful information that might be important at a later date (pun intended). Finally, use technology to your advantage and to build your relationship. You can connect through email, IM, DM, video chat or social media.

Why is a map important? A map will help you understand and differentiate between the countries of the United Kingdom. He might tell you he's British, but you can deconstruct this even further. You can start with something small like his accent. The British man's accent can tell you a great deal about him. For instance, if your man sounds like the actor James McAvoy or Iain Glen, chances are he's Scottish and not English. English accents, much like American ones, vary by geographical location. Think of how Ricky Gervais does not sound like Daniel Kaluuya, James Cordon or Damian Lewis. All Englishmen do not sound the same. For instance, Marcus Rashford, an English footballer from Manchester does not sound like Ian Wright, a former English footballer from London. I'll say more about this in Chapter 3 – Speaking English, but having a map will show you where he calls home, and knowing a little something about a man's hometown will give you something to talk about on your first date. You can say, "Tell me about the place you grew up." If he lives in a different place than where he grew up, you can say, "What's different about where you live now and where you spent your childhood?" If you have taken the time to learn about his nationality, you'll be starting your dating relationship in a good place.

My Beginning:

Dating has always been hard for me. I grew up in Michigan and attended Academy of the Sacred Heart, an all-girls Catholic High School in a suburb outside of Detroit. All my dates in high school had been arranged and my prom date was a guy from church. I think we were the same height and weight (he may have even been skinner than me). In college, I dated one man seriously for three years. After college, I moved to Philadelphia and tried to maintain my college relationship, but it was waning, as I was in Pennsylvania and he was in New York. In my last year of graduate school, I called off my engagement when I found out my fiancé was cheating on me with a woman I had considered a friend. A series of doomed relationships followed. Could it be that because I was educated, independent, semi-high maintenance, religious, worldly, confident and ambitious that men were afraid of me? Rather than change, compromise or lower my standards in order to find love, I simply stopped dating and looking for "Mr. Right".

Fast-forward to my second year of living in Los Angeles. Remember I said dating was hard? Well, dating in Los Angeles, a city full of beautiful people, was even more difficult, which is why I chose to focus on my work. I was in my 30's and still single. I loved my life in California. I lived in Venice, had a great job and my best friend from Michigan, Emily, lived 10 minutes away in Playa, but I was lonely. It was Emily who convinced me to try online dating. I can always remember her saying, "it's a fun way to meet guys." Internet dating in 2001 was in its infancy, and online dating sites were still free. I signed up on a site called "Excite Classifieds". It seemed like a painless way to meet men, plus I would be fulfilling my promise to Emily to give online dating a try. Although Emily assured me she had never encountered any problems, she gave me a few pointers – never use your real name in an ad, get a secondary email that you only use for online dating sites and post a picture that shows your full body but not close up, at a distance. Finally, never agree to meet for dinner or drinks as a first date.

Armed with this precautionary advice, I set up my ad:

Female Seeking Male: Long-term, 35 y/o, 5ft 1in. tall, Los Angeles, CA.

My nom de plume was "Sunshine Hendrix", also known as "hyacinth310". I chose Sunshine because I lived in "sunny" L.A., my name was "Hendrix", just spelled differently and I loved the Bill Withers song, "Ain't No Sunshine". My favourite spring flower was the hyacinth and the area code for my part of L.A. was 310. The picture I used for my profile had been taken a few years earlier at a party when I was in graduate school. I was wearing a skirt with poppies (this will be significant later) and a black turtleneck sweater. I had curls in my hair, black heels on and my teeth looked extraordinarily white and straight. My profile also stated that I liked men with accents. I had officially entered the world of modern dating. It still felt a little creepy because there were trolls out there and people pretending to be someone they were not. Yet, it beat going to bars or being set up with the other single person at a friend's wedding. Little did I know that this foray into the online world would just be the beginning of my journey. At the time, I had no idea the Internet would define the next 20 years of my life.

It was June 20th at 10:09 am that his first email came. It read, "This is a response to your advertisement on Excite Classifieds."

To: Hyacinth310
From: Rick
Subject: *Hi…. your ad.*

Well, I guess it's better to correspond so…. love to hear from you….me, white, English, easy going in LA for 6 months from August……. looking for a friend……love seems too much of a long shot.

Whatever…. would love to hear from you……if not….. good luck with your search!

Rick

I re-read the email and thought, he could be interesting, plus he's not even in the country yet, so I don't have to meet him in person! I crafted a response. My love affair with an Englishman was about to begin!

Is He English, British or Both?

Often when we travel, my significant other will overhear folks speaking and will proceed to ask total strangers, "Are you from the UK?" His success rate thus far has been 100%, as the strangers reply, "yes". He will then engage them further by asking, "What part?" I always smile during these encounters, as I know he is delighted to have found fellow compatriots. When this first started happening, I wondered why he would say "UK". It was only after having lived in England that I came to understand the nuances of when to use the terms Britain (referring to the mainland), Great Britain, United Kingdom or British (referring to citizenship). I'll come back to this later in the chapter. The history of the United Kingdom is fascinating and rich and well beyond the scope of this book. However, it is only prudent to provide some historical highlights that may be of interest to you and can be used to impress your English friends and future in-laws.

The United Kingdom is comprised of four countries. Each country is distinct and full of traditions and cultural norms unique to its region. The four countries of the United Kingdom (UK) are:

1. England
2. Scotland
3. Wales
4. Northern Ireland

The United Kingdom

Scotland

Northern Ireland

England

Wales

The flag of the United Kingdom is commonly referred to as the "Union Jack". It is sometimes, unintentionally, misrepresented as the English flag.

Interesting Flag Facts

The flag represents the union of the countries, and upon closer inspection one can see that it contains the red cross of St. George (the patron saint of England), the Cross of St. Patrick (the patron saint of Ireland) and the Saltire of St. Andrew (patron saint of Scotland). The flag, although appearing symmetric, is not. The white lines above and below the red diagonal are different widths. If the flag is rotated 180 degrees, it will not impact the design, but if the flag is viewed in a mirror, it will appear upside down. The only country flag not represented is that of Wales, which is subsumed by the English flag. People have been known to mistake the Union Jack as the flag of England.

The Union Flag has been traditionally flown on the official birthday of the ruling Monarch, Accession Day, Coronation Day, Commonwealth Day, Remembrance Sunday, the wedding anniversary of the Monarch, the days that mark the birth of royal family members and the Opening of Parliament. The flag is also flown in Wales on March 1st (St. David's Day), in Northern Ireland on St. Patrick's Day (March 17th), on

April 23rd in England (St. George's Day in England) and on November 30th (St. Andrew's Day in Scotland). Importantly, the Union Flag will only fly if there are two flagpoles.

Prior to July 2007, the Union Flag was only flown on Government buildings on a limited number of special days each year, determined by the Department for Culture, Media and Sport. In July 2007, this was changed when Prime Minister Gordon Brown announced that the Union Flag would fly 365 days a year above the front entrance of No. 10 Downing Street (the official office and residence of the Prime Minister). Other Government buildings were encouraged to do the same. The flag flies from Government buildings at half-mast when the death of the King or Queen is announced. It also flies at half-mast the day of the funeral of a member of the royal family or of a foreign ruler. Finally, it is flown at half-mast for the funeral of a former or current Prime Minister. The sovereign can also declare other occasions when the Union Flag is to be flown at half-mast. Additionally, there are the Royal Standard flags, which are personal flags used by the monarch on special occasions and to indicate if she is in residence at one of her royal palaces. The national anthem for the United Kingdom is "God Save the (insert the appropriate monarch – Queen or King)".

For your reference, I'll briefly describe each of the four countries that comprise the United Kingdom. The information may come in handy if your date turns out to be Scottish or Welsh and not English. In the next sections, the map, flag and a few historical facts and interesting highlights related to the specific country will be described. I'll start with England, the focal country of this book.

England

I like this map because it shows not only the regions of England (in colour), but also the major cities located within that region. Additionally, it shows the major transport hubs in the other parts of the UK (grey areas) and the Western tip of France. England is comprised of nine Government Regions: East of England, East Midlands, London, North East, South East, South West, North West, West Midlands, Yorkshire and the Heart of England or Humber. Over 80% of the total UK population lives in England.

Capital: London
Largest City: London
World Heritage Sites:

- Blenheim Palace
- Canterbury Cathedral
- City of Bath
- Cornwall & West Devon Mining Landscape
- Derwent Valley Mills
- Dorset and East Devon Coastline
- Durham Castle & Cathedral
- The Lake District
- Ironbridge Gorge
- Liverpool Maritime Mercantile City
- Saltaire
- Stonehenge
- Studley Royal Park

Four World Heritage sites are in London alone:

- The Tower of London
- The Palace of Westminster, Westminster Abbey
- Kew Royal Botanical Gardens
- Maritime Greenwich

Flag of England

Early in England's history, the three lions of the royal coat of arms were used as the flag of England. During the 13th century, the Cross of St. George was being used widely (in part, due to the first crusaders) and officially became the flag of England and Wales. Sometimes, the flag is mistakenly thought to be the Red Cross or Swiss flag; however, on those flags, the red cross does not extend to the edges as it does in the English flag. The history of England has been documented extensively in texts and historical novels. Therefore, I offer only a few of my favourite historical facts.

12 Interesting Facts & Highlights Related to Great Britain and England:

1. *Stonehenge* is a Neolithic and Bronze Age monument located in the county of Wiltshire. Archaeologists believe the structure was built sometime around 2200–2500 BC. It is thought that the site served as a burial and ceremonial ground in its heyday of 3000 BC.

It is one of the most visited tourist sites in England. Nearby, is the village of **Avebury**, which is surrounded by an older Neolithic site, but it is not quite as well-known as its neighbour to the north. To learn more visit: www. nationaltrust.org.uk/avebury

Avebury Stones

2. ***The Roman*** invasion of Britain can be traced to around 54 BC under Julius Caesar. Real occupation occurred around 43 AD under Emperor Claudius. The Roman influence can still be seen today in modern England in places such as the ***City of Bath*** or several of the straight Roman roads scattered throughout the country. I recommend taking a tour of the **Roman Baths** and then having lunch at the **Pump Room** before taking an afternoon tour of **Bath Abbey**. Bath is also home to the **Jane Austen Centre**. There is something for everyone in Bath.
http://www.romanbaths.co.uk/pump_room.aspx
https://www.janeausten.co.uk/

The Roman Baths

3.***Anglo-Saxon*** England came about at the end of Roman Britain as several Kingdoms (i.e., Kent, Sussex, East Anglia, Wessex, Northumbria). The Anglo-Saxons ruled the land until the Norman Conquest.

This map shows the kingdoms that comprised Great Britain circa 800. The colours indicate the ethnic groups at the time:

WESSEX: Anglo-Saxons (red)
GWYNEDD: Celts (grey)
FORTRIU: Picts (green).

4. ***1066 -*** The deciding Battle of Hastings resulted in the Norman conquest of England and William the Conqueror becoming King of England. You can visit the battlefield and Abbey in Sussex. As an English Heritage site, there is a visitor's centre and souvenir shop. For more information on admission to Battle Abbey and other English Heritage properties visit: http://www.englishheritage.org.uk/daysout/properties/1066-battle-of-hastings-abbeyand-battlefield/

5. ***The Magna Carta*** was first issued in 1215 and was signed into law in 1225. It was originally written by the barons of King John. There were several versions created over subsequent centuries. The 1297 version, ***The Great Charter of the Liberties of England, and of the Liberties of the Forest*** is still on the books in England. The significance of the Charter is that it serves as the basis for rule by Constitutional law.

6. ***The War of the Roses*** was fought between 1455 and 1487. This medieval civil war was between the Houses of Lancaster and York. The White Rose signified the House of York. The Red Rose belonged to the House of Lancaster.

The Lancastarian, Henry Tudor established the House of Tudor. The Tudors were victorious in this civil war, and the House of Tudor ruled England and Wales for over 100 years. The Tudor Rose, which is a combination of both roses, became the national flower of England and was a symbol of peace.

7. *The "Elizabeth" Queens:*
   Queen Elizabeth I defeated the Spanish Armada in 1588. Elizabeth was the daughter of King Henry VIII and Anne Boleyn. She was the last Tudor monarch.

   Queen Elizabeth II is from the House of Windsor. Her father, King George VI became the monarch when his brother Edward VIII, abdicated the throne in order to marry an American divorcee. Queen Elizabeth II will most likely be the longest reigning monarch to sit on the English throne, surpassing Queen Victoria's 63-years of British reign.

8. *The Battle of Trafalgar* was a pivotal sea battle between the British Royal Navy and the combined Spanish and French Navies. This decisive victory for the British was led by Admiral Horatio Nelson. Nelson's flagship, the **HMS Victory**, can be seen by visitors and is dry-docked in Portsmouth. It is part of the National Museum of the Royal Navy.

   Nelson's monument is located in *Trafalgar Square*, one of the most visited squares in central London. When you're in the Square, you can see the clock tower of Big Ben in the distance.

Trafalgar Square

9. ***World Wars I & II*** – The First World War took place between 1914 and 1918. The Second World War took place between the years of 1939 and 1945. In both wars, Britain was engaged in battle against Germany. ***Winston Leonard Spencer Churchill***, the British Prime Minister during WWII was not only a great statesman but also a great orator and in 1940 made one of the most memorable speeches to the House of Commons in which he stated, "*we shall defend our Island, whatever the cost may be, we shall fight on the beaches, we shall fight on the landing grounds, we shall fight in the fields and in the streets, we shall fight in the hills; we shall never surrender*". If you are visiting London and you are a war buff or historian, you might enjoy Churchill's War Rooms. Visit the ***Imperial War Museums*** site, http://www.iwm.org.uk/visits/churchill-war-rooms, for more details.

10. ***Lady Diana Spencer marries Charles, Prince of Wales*** and becomes Princess Diana in 1981. Their wedding was watched by millions around the world. Although the couple divorced in 1995, they did manage to provide the

Queen with two more grandsons, Princes William and Harry. Tragically, Diana died in an automobile accident in Paris in 1997.

11. ***HRH Prince William***, the first-born son of Prince Charles and Diana, Princess of Wales, married Kate Middleton in April 2011. In a touching act worth noting, Prince William gave Catherine his mother's engagement ring. The future King and Queen Consort of England seem to appeal to old and young alike. Their modern family attitude is quite refreshing. The Duchess of Cambridge – Kate's title now – was not from an aristocratic family and was not forced to marry into the British Royal family. It appears the couple genuinely fell in love. Their future looks bright, as they are proud parents to three really cute children. Who can forget the image of young Prince George meeting former President Barack Obama and former First Lady Michelle in his pajamas!

12. ***The Duke and Duchess of Sussex*** – Well, this is the appropriate conclusion to this section on England. The Duchess of Sussex, the former Ms. Markle is a modern American woman personified. She married her charming Prince Harry and brought to the relationship not only beauty, brains and her own money but also a sense of purpose (her charity work) and multiple identities (American, Californian, daughter, biracial, divorcée, friend). Millions of Americans woke up extremely early to watch her televised wedding ceremony (me included) to the handsome Prince. Everything about their wedding day was beautiful – the bride, the bride's mother, the dress, the ceremony, the music, the weather and the guests. I am happy to welcome this couple to *The Modern American Woman and The Englishman* club!

Scotland

Map Courtesy of Google Maps

Scotland is the northern-most country of the United Kingdom. It borders England to the South. It is bound by the North Sea on the east and the Atlantic Ocean on the west. Interestingly, the geography of Scotland is comprised of over 700 islands.

Capital: Edinburgh
Largest City: Glasgow
World Heritage Sites:

- Neolithic Orkney
- The Antonine Wall
- Towns of Edinburgh

- St Kilda
- The Forth Bridge
- New Lanark

Flag of Scotland

The flag of Scotland is also known as St. Andrew's Cross or The Saltire. The white cross represents the crucifixion cross of St. Andrew, and it is placed on a sky-blue field. St. Andrew is the patron Saint of Scotland. He is celebrated on November 30, which is a national holiday in Scotland.

11 Interesting Facts & Highlights Related to Scotland:

1. ***The Caledonians*** resisted the Roman invasion in 43 BC as much as they could. It is believed that people lived for thousands of years in Scotland prior to their history being recorded by the Romans. Fortified settlements date back to the Iron Age. Organized settlement ruins have been found in the Orkney and Shetland Islands. ***The Picts*** were the original people of the country and occupied most of Scotland north of the Firth of Clyde and the Firth of Forth. In the 6th century, Gaelic-speaking people came to the Highlands and prevailed in wars with the Picts.

2. **Hadrian's Wall** maintained the border between the southern Roman-occupied territory and northern Scotland. It was built to prevent raids on Roman Britain by the Pictish tribes of the North. It was made a UNESCO World Heritage Site in 1987. Sections of the military fortification built by the Romans under Emperor Hadrian still exist; it is commonly referred to as the "Roman Wall".

3. **Knap of Howar** is the oldest standing house in Northern Europe, dating from 3500 BC. It is located in Papa Westray on Orkney Island. **Skara Brae** is an example of the stone houses built by Neolithic farmers in Scotland. To experience this prehistoric village, go to www.historic-scotland.gov.uk. **The Fortingall Yew** can be found in the churchyard in the village of Fortingall. It is believed to be the oldest tree in Europe at 2,000 years old.

4. **Tartan** is the most familiar pattern of cloth associated with Scotland. The crisscross pattern is known as plaid in America. Originally, local weavers used wool to make the pattern, and the tartan was associated with regions of Scotland. In the nineteenth century, the tartan became associated with Scottish clans or families. A division of the military, the Black Watch or The Royal Highland Regiment, has a tartan of its own. This pattern is probably one of the most recognized tartans in the world. I love my Englishman, but there is something quite special about a man in a kilt!

5. ***The Kingdom of Scotland*** was united in 843 and remained independent until the Act of the Union in 1707, which joined the Kingdoms of Scotland and England. William Wallace led resistance to English occupation of Scotland but was eventually captured and then drawn and quartered in London in 1305. In 1746, Bonnie Prince Charlie was defeated, and with that defeat, the attempt to restore the Catholic Stuarts to the Throne ended.

6. ***Peaty Nectar,*** also known as whisky, can be found all over the country. Scotland is famous for its distilleries. There are many opportunities to tour a distillery and sample some peaty nectar. To learn more about the Scotch whisky-making process and discover the various varieties of whisky, visit www.whisky-heritage.co.uk

7. ***Lochs*** are bodies of water found throughout Scotland. The word "loch" originates from the Scottish Gaelic word for lake. The most famous Scottish loch is "Ness" for its presumed containment of the water monster. Other lochs include Loch Lomond (the largest), Loch Morar, Loch Awe, Loch Maree and Loch Katrine. For more information, visit www.lochlomond-trossachs.org

8. ***Mary Queen of Scots*** was born to King James V of Scotland in 1542. Her father died in 1543, and Mary was crowned Queen even though she was only a baby. During Mary's lifetime, she faced political plotting, religious unrest, marital trouble, family in-fighting and imprisonment. She had one son, James, born in 1566. In 1586, Mary was tried for crimes against her cousin, Queen Elizabeth I of England, and executed. In a strange twist of fate, when Elizabeth died in 1603, Mary's son, King James VI of Scotland, became King James I of England. James was the first King of Scotland and England. In an act of contrition for treating his mother

so poorly during her lifetime, James moved his mother's body to Westminster Abbey in London, where her magnificent marble tomb remains.

9. Several domesticated **dog breeds** have originated from Scotland. The most well-known are probably in the terrier family. You might recognize the names: Scottish Dandie, Skye Terrier, the Westie and the Cairn (Toto from Wizard of Oz).

10. **Two Scottish Castles:**
    Dunnottar Castle – The site where the castle ruins now stand are thought to have been a Pictish fortress. The castle holds an interesting place in Scottish history, not only because of its dramatic landscape but also because it has been the site of many battles and once provided haven to the Scottish Crown Jewels. The castle sits high upon a natural rock that is surrounded by the North Sea on three sides. It is south of Stonehaven in Aberdeenshire and can only be accessed by a narrow strip of land.

Dunnottar Castle

Huntly Castle, located a few miles outside of the current town of Huntly, is now in ruins, but it also has an interesting history, and the ruins are quite impressive. In contrast to Dunnottar, it is located inland and was rebuilt, destroyed, burned down and rebuilt over and over again. For an exciting day out in Scotland, go castle exploring: https://www.dunnottarcastle.co.uk/

For more information on Huntly Castle, go to the undiscovered Scotland website: www.undiscoveredscotland.co.uk/huntly/huntlycastle/index.html

If you go to Huntly, I suggest staying at the Castle Hotel, Huntly, it is a welcoming, friendly hotel (http://www.castlehotel.uk.com/). Richard and I were delayed at Heathrow on a flight to Scotland, and we ended up arriving late in the evening. We called the hotel to let them know we were still coming. Despite the fact that the kitchen was closed, and dinner service was long over by the time we arrived, they had sandwiches waiting for us and a stiff whisky for Richard. We sat and ate our sandwiches in the bar, which was cosy and relaxing after a long day of travelling.

11. ***Edinburgh*** is the 2nd most visited tourist city in the UK. It is the seat of the Scottish Parliament and each August is host to one of the world's largest performing arts festivals, *The Edinburgh Festival*. The *Royal Edinburgh Military Tattoo* is one of the many highlights of the festival. It's hard not to appreciate the wonderful bagpipe playing that is on display during this time.

Historic Edinburgh city street

Wales

Map Courtesy of Google Maps

Wales is situated to the west of England and is bound by the Atlantic Ocean and Irish Sea. The Welsh coastline is dramatic and beautiful. The landscape changes from rocky cliffs to sandy beaches.

Flag of Wales/Cymru

The Welsh National flag's most prominent feature is its red dragon, which is placed on a white and green field. The dragon represents the Red Dragon of Cadwaladr, King of Gwynedd, along with the other Tudor colours of green and white. The flag was used by Henry VII in 1485 during the Bosworth Field battle; it became the official flag of Wales in 1959.

Capital: Cardiff
Largest City: Cardiff
Languages: English & Welsh

"Y ddraig goch ddyry cychwyn" – The Red Dragon will lead the way.

World Heritage Sites:

- Blaenavon Industrial Landscape
- Castles and Town Walls of King Edward in Gwynedd
- Pontcysyllte Aqueduct and Canal

National Anthem: *Hen Wlad fy Nhadau* – Land of My Fathers

11 Interesting Facts & Highlights Related to Wales:

1. ***Blaenavon*** –Wales was the leading producer of iron and coal in the 19th century, and the area was known for its mass production of these materials. It is now a World Heritage site.

2. ***Edward I*** built magnificent castles. Indeed, his Castles in Gwynedd and Town Walls are legendary. Edward was also the first English monarch to crown his son, born in 1284 at Caernarfon Castle, the "Prince of Wales". In 1969, Queen Elizabeth II crowned her son, Charles, Prince of Wales.

3. Seven **Northern Welsh landmarks** were written anonymously into the following rhyme:

Pistyll Rhaeadr and Wrexham steeple, Snowdon's mountain without its people, Overton yew trees, St Winefride wells, Llangollen bridge and Gresford bells.

Pistyll Rhaeadr is the tallest waterfall in England & Wales.

4. The ***daffodil*** is the national flower of Wales and is typically worn on March 1st, St. David's Day. The ***leek*** is one of the national symbols of Wales.

5. ***Snowdon Mountain Railway*** offers a scenic view of Snowdonia National Park while riding an old-fashioned steam train. Snowdon Mountain has the highest peak in Britain. For something other than your traditional bus tour try the train: www.snowdonrailway.co.uk

6. ***Portmeirion Village*** was the picturesque vision of Sir Charles Williams-Ellis. He created a coastal retreat reminiscent of a small Italian village. You may also recognize the name Portmeirion from the pottery collection his daughter started selling in the village gift shop. Portmeirion china is famous for its beautiful floral designs. For more information visit: http://www.portmeirion-village.com/

7. ***St. David's Cathedral*** in Pembrokeshire was built on the site of St. David's original monastery. The Cathedral is open for tours, and the refractory serves local food. Saint David is the patron saint of Wales, and his flag is often flown on March 1st, St. David's Day. http://www.stdavidscathedral.org.uk/

8. ***Music*** plays a critical role in Welsh culture. The Welsh are famous for their choirs, musicians and singers. The Millennium Centre in Cardiff is a contemporary building that showcases the rich musical heritage of Wales. Find out what's on offer by visiting: www.wmc.org.uk

9. ***The Welsh National Assembly*** is relatively new, having only been enacted in 1998. Moreover, it was only in 2011 that Assembly members were able to pass legislation without deferring to the UK Parliament. ***The Senedd*** is the Assembly's environmentally conscious chamber house. It was built using traditional Welsh materials. The Senedd opened in 2006 on St. David's Day. For more information, visit: http://assemblywales.org/

10. ***The Welsh Guard*** was established in 1915 by King George V to complete the foot guards associated with the countries of the United Kingdom (i.e., the English Grenadiers & Coldstream Guards, the Irish Guards and the Scots Guards). They are famous for their red coats and (American black) bearskin hats. In addition to serving in the active military, the Welsh Guards also perform ceremonial and public duties. They are part of the Foot Guards Regiment and guard the Queen at her royal residencies. The first King's guard at Buckingham Palace was mounted on March 1, 1915 (St. David's Day, of course).

11. ***BBC Cymru*** is the Welsh language FM radio station that began broadcasting in 1977. Radio Cymru became available online in 2005. Take a listen at www.bbc.co.uk/radiocymru

Northern Ireland

Map Courtesy of Google Maps

Capital: Belfast
Languages: English and Irish Gaelic
Largest City: Belfast
World Heritage Site:

- Giant's Causeway

The Union Jack is the flag that is flown by the British government in Northern Ireland, as it is the official flag of Great Britain and Northern Ireland. There is no other "officially sanctioned" flag of Northern Ireland. The Ulster Banner was used until 1972.

11 Interesting Facts & Highlights Related to Northern Ireland:

1. ***The Six Counties*** of Northern Ireland were used for governmental purposes from 1921 to 1972. The counties are Antrim, Londonderry, Tyrone, Fermanagh, Armagh and Down. The counties no longer represent local political divisions, and instead the country is divided into twenty-six council areas. The counties are now primarily used to explain or describe locations. Although Northern Ireland is the smallest country in the United Kingdom, there is plenty to do and see there.

2. ***Saint Patrick*** is the patron Saint of Ireland. He spent his childhood in Roman Britain. At the age of sixteen, he was kidnapped and taken to Ireland, where he was enslaved for six years. He managed to escape by boat back to Britain. Patrick had become deeply religious during his time in Ireland and decided the best way to serve God was to become a priest. After seminary, Patrick

returned to Ireland and began to convert druidic pagans
to Catholicism. Patrick built a monastery in Armagh,
and it became the Christian learning centre in Ireland. St.
Patrick is believed to be buried in the grounds at Down
Cathedral, Downpatrick. For more information visit
http://www.saintpatrickcentre.com/

3. *The Titanic* was one of the more famous ocean liners
   built in the shipyards of Belfast by the shipping company
   White Star.

4. *Carrick-a-Rede Rope Bridge* was originally used by
   fishermen to check their nets. It is now used by tourists to
   experience the magnificent views of the coast.

5. *Giant's Causeway* is Northern Ireland's World Heritage
   Site. This coastal landscape is also part of a National
   Nature Reserve. www.nationaltrust.org.uk/giantscauseway

6. ***Old Bushmills*** distillery located in County Antrim has been producing whiskey for over 400 years. The distillery offers tours to the public. No trip to Northern Ireland would be complete without a wee bit of this classic Irish dram. For more information, visit www.bushmills.com

7. ***The Ulster American Folk Park***, located in Omagh, describes how many Irish emigrated from the Ulster area to America in the 18th and 19th centuries. The Park is part of the National Museums of Northern Ireland, which also include the Ulster Museum, The Ulster Folk & Transport Museum and the Armagh County Museum. Information on the Folk Park can be found at https://www.nmni.com/our-museums/ulster-american-folkpark/Home.aspx

8. ***The Walled City of Londonderry***, also known as **Derry**, is the only walled city in Northern Ireland. The Walls of Derry were built between 1613 and 1618 as protection from the Scottish and English. The Walls provide unique insight into the original design and street plan of the town, which still exists today.

9. ***The Troubles*** date from 1968 to 1998. These years mark the thirty years of civil unrest between the Unionists and Nationalists. Flags (Union, Ulster Banner or Tri-colour) and wall murals let you know which you were entering or leaving.

Paramilitary groups formed and would engage in civil disobedience and armed attacks on those who opposed their views. The height of the conflict came in 1972 with what became known as the "Bloody Sunday" attack, in which unarmed civilians were killed in Derry. In 1998, the Belfast Agreement (The Good Friday Agreement) was signed in an attempt to end the violence and political fighting. The University of Ulster has established the **CAIN Web Service** (http://cain.ulst.ac.uk/), which documents the conflict in Northern Ireland from this time period. CAIN is an acronym for Conflict Archive on the INternet. The mural above is taken from the *Mural Directory* (located on the CAIN website*)* compiled by Dr. Jonathan McCormick, who has photographed, and catalogued murals located throughout Northern Ireland. http://cain.ulst.ac.uk/bibdbs/murals/index.html

10. ***Parliament Buildings*** in Belfast is where the Northern Ireland Assembly meets to make legislative decisions. The

Northern Ireland Assembly was established as a result of the Good Friday Agreement (Belfast Agreement) in 1998. During the summer months, visitors can tour the Assembly and Senate Chambers and, after their tour, enjoy a picnic on the Stormont Estate.

11. An ***Ulster Fry*** is a breakfast meal that typically consists of eggs, bacon, sausages, black pudding, potato bread and soda farls (soda bread, prepared in a skillet and cut into 4 equal parts).

The statement that the "sun never set upon the British Empire" was true at the height of British imperial rule. However, after the Second World War, the British Empire was gradually dismantled. India, former African territories, such as Rhodesia, several Caribbean islands and Hong Kong (in 1997) became independent of British rule. Many former colonies became part of the Commonwealth of Nations, which is a non-political, voluntary association. To date, the following members of the Commonwealth share their heads of state with the UK including:

Canada
Australia
New Zealand
Papua New Guinea
Saint Kitts & Nevis
Saint Lucia
Barbados
Saint Vincent & the Grenadines
Solomon Islands
Belize
Tuvalu
The Bahamas
Jamaica
Antigua and Barbuda

So, there you have it, a brief introduction to the countries that make up the United Kingdom. In the beginning of the chapter, I told you I would come back to the subtleties of referencing British, Great Britain or UK. It can be confusing to remember when to use what name. The term "British" connotes the beliefs, customs and political ideals (e.g., the crown as a unifying symbol) that all four countries have in common. The term "Great Britain" includes not just the mainland but also the Channel Islands, Northern Ireland and the Isle of Man. Typically, when referring to citizenship, people will say, "British"; however, if asked about nationality, they will reply "Welsh" or "Scottish" etc. There is a strong sense of national identity and this is often reflected in sport. My solution is to ask the person when in doubt. Richard sometimes says "English", and sometimes when in America he says "British". When we are in England, people hear his accent and automatically know he is from the Western part of England, known as the "West Country".

My Advice: Know your man's national identity. If you are unsure, the best way to find out is to simply ask him.

CHAPTER 2

Once in England, Where Exactly are you?

 PART I

I first thought about calling this chapter "Location, Location, Location" and then "Know Your Places". It was my attempt at trying to have a clever chapter title, but neither was right. So, you get the boring title printed above instead. In this chapter, I really want to highlight how important your location and the sense of place are in England. There is an adage that says, "*where you stand, determines what you see, who you listen to, determines what you hear*". Although I first read this from a philosophical and slightly political perspective, I have found it useful in the literal sense, particularly in England and other parts of the British Isles. There are so many beautiful, majestic and magical places to live, visit and explore, from the farmland of Devon to the Lake District, from the urbanity of Bristol to the picturesque village of Castle Combe. England is comprised of large cities (think Manchester) as well as small cities (think Stoke-on-Trent), towns and villages. Defining why a place is either a city, town, village or hamlet has to do with a combination of history, charter status, population and services. For instance, when I first moved to England, I lived in Frome, which is a historical market *town* in Somerset. It is close to Mells, which has a church, tithe barn and a traditional coaching inn and pub and is referred to as a *village*. The World Heritage *city* of Bath, with its abbey and universities, is located only a few miles away. You can wake up in the city and drive to the beautiful countryside or seaside for a day trip. I haven't even mentioned seaside towns such as, Brighton, Torquay, Great Yarmouth, or Weymouth. I'm putting the map in this chapter again for easy reference.

I have compiled a list of English cities you may already know about and want to visit (in alphabetical order), not in order of preference, although two of my favourite cities are Bath and Bristol. Actually, it is quite difficult to say I have a favourite city because there is something special about each of these places. My sense of history comes to me when I go to Plymouth, as it is from there the Pilgrim fathers and mothers sailed to

America, not knowing what they would find or if they would survive. When I think of Oxford and Cambridge, I think of great crew rivalries (just kidding). These two university cities are steeped in rich, scholarly history, but they have much to offer to academics and non-academics alike.

The cathedral in Wells is one of the prettiest I have visited, yet the cathedral in Salisbury has a copy of the *Magna Carta*. The city of Liverpool is a favourite for both us. For Richard, it is the football, the Beatles museum and the Grand National. For me, it is the cultural history of the city I find fascinating – it was part of the Atlantic slave trade and the former home to the Cunard and White Star (think Titanic) shipping lines. Truro was my first stop in Cornwall. It's a city, but it doesn't overwhelm you. As you can see, it is hard to have a favourite. My suggestion is to visit them all! Here's the list:

- Bath
- Birmingham
- Bradford
- Brighton and Hove
- Bristol
- Cambridge
- Canterbury
- Carlisle
- Chester
- Chichester
- Coventry
- Derby
- Durham
- Ely
- Exeter
- Gloucester
- Hereford
- Kingston upon Hull
- Lancaster
- Leeds

- Leicester
- Lichfield
- Lincoln
- Liverpool
- London
- Manchester
- Newcastle upon Tyne
- Norwich
- Nottingham
- Oxford
- Peterborough
- Plymouth
- Portsmouth
- Preston
- Ripon
- Salford
- Salisbury
- Sheffield
- Southampton
- St Albans
- Stoke-on- Trent
- Sunderland
- Truro
- Wakefield
- Wells
- Westminster
- Winchester
- Wolverhampton
- Worcester
- York

As you explore England, it might also be helpful to know the county names in addition to the city, town or village name. You can impress your new beau with your level of knowledge about his home county. Here is an alphabetized list of English Counties:

- Bedfordshire
- Berkshire
- Buckinghamshire
- Cambridgeshire
- Cheshire
- City of London
- Cornwall
- Cumbria
- Derbyshire
- Devon
- Dorset
- Durham
- East Riding of Yorkshire
- East Sussex
- Essex
- Gloucestershire
- Greater London
- Greater Manchester
- Hampshire
- Herefordshire
- Hertfordshire
- Isle of Wight
- Kent
- Lancashire
- Leicestershire Lincolnshire
- Merseyside
- Norfolk
- North Yorkshire
- Northamptonshire
- Northumberland
- Nottinghamshire
- Oxfordshire
- Rutland
- Shropshire
- Somerset
- South Yorkshire

- Staffordshire
- Suffolk
- Surrey
- Tyne and Wear
- Warwickshire
- West Midlands
- West Sussex
- West Yorkshire
- Wiltshire
- Worcestershire

Quick Tip 1: Here's how I make an educated guess of whether I'm in a city, town, hamlet or village:

Is it a sprawling metropolis with frequent train and bus (including open-top tour) service? A football (soccer) team or teams? A university? A cathedral or abbey? **Is it hard to find parking?** Do I have to pay to park? – I'm most likely in a city.

Does it have a dedicated market day? A council? A few churches? Several pubs? Shopping in the centre? A library? Does it have a cricket pitch? **Is it hard to find parking?** – I'm probably in a town.

Is it picturesque, with no services that can been seen? Does it have cottages with thatched roofs? **Is there limited parking?** If I close my eyes for five minutes will I have driven through it? – I'm probably in a hamlet.

Is it pretty and small, with one shop that also doubles as a post office? Does it have one church, one hall and a pub? Is the main street lined with quaint cottages? **Are parking spaces limited?** – I'm probably in a village.

PART II

Getting Around and Finding your way: Transportation & Travel

So, now that you are ready to explore the English counties, what's the best way to get there? When I first moved to England, I didn't have a car, nor did I feel comfortable driving on the left side of the road. Richard secured a bus pass for me. I learned my way around Somerset and Bristol because of riding a double decker bus.

Did you notice a common theme in **Quick Tip 1** had to do with the difficulty of parking? I suggest, as much as possible, to try and explore England without a car. There are various modes of transportation other than a car that make getting around the country easy – buses, trains, boats, airplanes, bikes and horses are all viable alternatives.

Buses

Buses and coaches are used by people throughout the country to get to work, school or a holiday destination. You can take day-long or weekend coach trips. There are weekday and weekend schedules, which make it easy to go shopping in the city centre or get to work on time. As I mentioned earlier, prior to driving in England, I would ride the bus into work. It was a double decker, and I would sit on the top deck, which allowed me to see the lay of the land. These journeys prepared me quite well for driving, as I knew where the road was heading and when to expect a bend, stoplight or cow crossing. I was always amazed at how astutely the bus driver was able to navigate those narrow country roads. The bus is an affordable way to travel within your familiar environs or throughout the UK. Bus passes of various durations (1-day, 7-day, monthly etc.) are usually available for purchase, typically at a staffed bus station or online. You'll see the following large bus companies operating in England and throughout the UK: *FirstGroup, Arriva, Stagecoach* and *National Express.*

Trains

For me, the exciting way to travel in England and around the UK is by train. I find riding the train to be quite an enjoyable experience. After I moved out to the countryside, I commuted into London for a year on the train. I would grab a bacon sandwich, a cup of tea and the newspaper and I was all set for my workday journey. The train system is geared up to get travellers and commuters where they need to go. *The National Rail Service* coordinates the network of train services in England and throughout the UK. Depending on where you are in the country, the train lines are run by different rail operators. Typically, there are two class services offered: standard and first-class. Although it does depend on the route, first-class may not be available on all routes. If you are going to take your bike on the train, it is worth checking ahead of time to see if there are bike storage facilities on board and if you need to make reservations for your bike. The following is an alphabetical list and brief description of the primary train operators you may encounter whilst travelling in the country.

Arriva Trains operates in Wales and services all the major train stations (Cardiff, Swansea and Newport), where you can then connect to other operators for service to cities in England.

C2C Rail is owned by National Express and offers limited service from London to places in Essex and Southend-on-Sea

Chiltern Railways services select cities between London and Birmingham.

CrossCountry Trains, as the name implies, offers train service across the UK from Penzance to Edinburgh.

Docklands Light Railway (DLR) is operated by the Transport of London and connects parts of London with the Docklands.

East Coast is a partnership between Virgin Trains and Stagecoach and offers rail service that links cities in the North with cities in the eastern part of the country.

East Midlands Trains operates trains from cities in the East Midlands (Nottingham, Derby etc.) to London. It also offers train service from Northern cities (Liverpool, Leeds etc.) to London.

Eurostar offers travellers fast rail service from London to France and Belgium. Eurostar has many city breaks that are affordable and time efficient.

First Capital Connect, as the name suggests, connects travellers to various locations within the capital city of London and a few beyond.

Gatwick Express has non-stop rail service from Gatwick Airport to London's Victoria Station. It also has connecting services to get you from Gatwick to Brighton.

Great Western is operated by FirstGroup. They primarily service the western part of the country and offer frequent, high-speed service from London Paddington to most regional station hubs in the South West (Bristol, Swansea, Cardiff, Penzance and Plymouth).

Heathrow Express offers convenient, non-stop rail service from Heathrow Airport to London Paddington Station.

London Overground is not as well-known as its underground cousin, but it offers passengers access to a conurbation of cities surrounding the capital.

London Underground (also known as "The Tube") is legendary, with its easily identifiable and iconic underground symbol. It is the fastest way to travel around the city of London. You can buy passes or purchase an Oyster card for ease.

Merseyrail provides services to those travelling in the Merseyside or Liverpool regions.

National Express East Anglia trains, as the name suggests, offers rail service in the East, servicing such cities as Cambridge, Peterborough, Norwich and Great Yarmouth on the east coast.

Northern Rail provides passengers rail service throughout the North of England. Cities such as Manchester, York, Blackpool and Liverpool connect with other northern towns and cities, such as Carlisle, Grismby, Nottingham, Sunderland and Chester.

South West Trains offers service from London's Waterloo station to cities in the southwest of England, such as Exeter St Davids, Portsmouth, Yeovil and Weymouth.

Southeastern Trains, as the name implies, runs in the east of England, operating in the regions of East Sussex and Kent, calling at stations including Crawley, Hastings, Maidstone and Folkestone.

First Scot Rail offers commuters and travellers alike express service to major Scottish cities (e.g. Aberdeen, Glasgow, Inverness) with connections to Newcastle and Carlisle in

England. Sleeper cars are available from Edinburgh to London but need to be reserved in advance.

Virgin Trains offers services to major (primarily northern and southern) cities throughout the UK, operating from their London-based hub at Euston Station.

> **Quick Tip 2:** I suggest making a reservation for long train journeys (more than an hour) or if riding the train during peak times of the day. I also recommend avoiding the train during bank holidays, as that is typically the time the train operators do major engineering work.

Boats

Another way to travel (and live) is on a boat. England has water around it and through it, so, despite not being as fast or economical as a bus or train, boats do offer another way to travel within and out of the country. It is common to see narrowboats navigating their way through the English canal system. Narrowboats can be rented and can come equipped with a full and kitchen, although scaled down to fit the width of the canal. For those of you who have watched the television show *Peaky Blinders*, think of Tommy travelling from Birmingham to London on a canal boat. It took a few days, but he got there. If you have the time to explore, a canal boat holiday might be the way to go. You can discover quaint waterside villages, beautiful countryside and cities rich in history along the way to your final destination. If you do consider taking a boat through the canals, be sure to plan for the locks, which can be numerous. Of course, along the coast there are more traditional fishing boats and commercial vessels.

Ferries are a common way to get you out of England, with the most well-known ports being Dover (sail to France) and

Southampton (sail to America). However, there are several less famous ports that shuttle the English back and forth from place to place. Here is a list of ferry routes to and from England you may want to consider:

- England to the Isle of Man
- England to the Isle of Wight
- England to Jersey
- England to the Isles of Scilly
- England to Belgium
- England to Northern Ireland
- England to Holland
- England to Spain
- England to Ireland
- England to France

Airplanes

A quick way to travel is by plane. A flight from Bristol to Manchester is twenty minutes as opposed to 2–3 hours in the car. London Heathrow is one of the busiest airports in the world. Chances are you flew into it (or Gatwick) when coming over from America. I have listed a few of the other major airports in England below, but there are smaller regional airports that may be more practical to use depending upon where you are in the country.

1. London Gatwick
2. Luton
3. Stansted
4. Manchester
5. Birmingham
6. Liverpool
7. Bristol

In addition to the major airlines, which offer frequent services to international destinations, there are several low-cost, budget airlines that offer travellers an affordable way to leave the island.

Bicycles

Cycling can be a great way to see the country and exercise at the same time. There are idyllic routes throughout England where cyclists can either peddle right to the beach or the local pub. The *National Cycle Network* was created to provide cyclists with traffic-free paths to enjoy in England and throughout the UK.

Horses

Living in the stunning countryside, I frequently come across bridle paths. There are equestrian routes and trails positioned all over the country for riding enthusiasts. The *National Trails* website offers trail information and updates to riders, walkers and cyclists. The *British Horse Society* also provides ride maps, but it always a good idea to check the current conditions of a planned route.

Walking

I have found that probably one of the best ways to get around and enjoy England is to walk. Walking is free and allows easy access to places where other modes of transport just can't go! You can walk in the city or on dedicated walking paths. You can walk through gardens (think Kensington), up hills (think Glastonbury Tor), through woodlands, on coastal paths and over bridges. However, don't think that walkers are aimless day trippers. Ramblers and hikers can be quite serious in England,

and footpaths are used on a regular basis. If you want to take your Englishman on a walking holiday, why not give the folks at *Foot Trails* a ring? You can select from their current menu of tours, or they can design a romantic, bespoke walk in the South West for you. The famous Chinese proverb states, "*The journey of a thousand miles begins with a single step*".

You can be assured that your Englishman has travelled outside of England. Unlike folks at home in America, it is hard to find an English person who has never been out of England. Remember, he has the other countries of the United Kingdom at his doorstep. The European continent is only a short distance away, so it is likely that he has been out of his home country many times, whether for holiday or a school trip. As an example, Richard remembers going skiing in Switzerland for a school trip. My exotic school trip was going to the Detroit Zoo (which was a fantastic day out, by the way). The English travel to foreign countries frequently for sun and fun! Rumour has it that old English gangsters retire to places like Marbella, Spain (the weather there is lovely all year round, so I can understand the appeal). I think travelling in England (and Europe) is relatively easy. As you can see from reading this chapter, a romantic weekend in France can begin with catching the Eurostar at St. Pancras Station or taking the ferry from Dover to Calais. A train ride to the Lake District may be more enticing, or a walk along the coast may cause you to be reflective and contemplative. There are so many scenic and charming places in the UK to visit and experience, it isn't necessary to travel far. Whatever the case, I hope you now have a better sense of where you are in the country and where you can go! Have fun exploring together!

CHAPTER 3

Speaking "English"

Before moving to England, I thought (naively) that everyone in England sounded like the newscasters on BBC America. I had been to London on *holiday* (vacation) and was able to *get on* fine. On that first trip, I never ventured out of the greater London area. I now know having lived and worked in England that I speak "American" and my husband speaks "English" (albeit with a slight West Country accent). One of my *favourite* (spelled the English way) things to do when I am in England is to just sit back and listen to my husband and his mates (English term for friends) or family carry on a conversation. The Bristol brogue is not everyone's cup of tea, but it does make me smile when I hear it. I like the West Country accent because it sounds friendly, warm and is gentle on the ear. If the accent is too broad then I do have to strain a bit to understand, but after all these years, it still makes me smile.

In this chapter, I only highlight a few of the nuances in British English, so that you are not caught off guard when someone speaks to you or worse, make the mistake I made of pretending to understand when you really don't. Here is my embarrassing story of not understanding the English language. When I first moved to England, we had a lovely housekeeper named Diane. She had a fantastic Somerset accent, and for the most part I understood her. At one point in the year, a holiday was coming up, maybe Easter? I can't remember exactly, but it was either a Spring or Summer holiday, and I knew Diane would not be at work for a week or so. I preceded to ask her what she would be doing for the holiday or if she would be travelling, and she said, "Oh we're going to *Ourgaten Painten*". I replied, "Oh that will be nice". She looked at me and smiled and then carried on with her work. I had no idea where *Ourgaten Painten* was or if it was even in England. Later, when Richard arrived home from work, I told him the story and he started laughing while asking, "You said what?" I couldn't understand what was so funny. "Where is it? I've never heard of it before." I was starting to get annoyed that he was finding the story so amusing and not letting me in on the joke. Clearly, he knew something about this place.

"Poppy, this is what people say when they aren't going anywhere and just staying home." Richard's nickname for me was "Poppy". (He had decided to call me that after seeing the red and black poppy skirt I had worn in my profile picture when we first met online.) He then broke apart what she had said – *our gate*, meaning, we are only going as far as our front gate, and *painting*, meaning, maybe doing some stuff around the house. I had mistakenly heard all of the words combined due to the West Country accent and came up with a non-existent place called *Ourgaten Painten*. It was from this encounter that I learned to always ask if I didn't understand. This chapter is not an English–American dictionary or a pronunciation guide; rather, it is a practical introduction to some of the everyday differences in speech and language you will encounter *whilst* in the UK. You will start to recognise these dialects, accents and quirky British idioms as you travel to different parts of the United Kingdom. You will find that within the countries of the United Kingdom, the Scots speak English with a Scottish accent, the Welsh speak English with a Welsh accent and the Northern Irish speak English with a Northern Irish accent. In Wales or Cymru, both Welsh and English are spoken. Signs are posted in both languages, there is a BBC Wales channel and it is not uncommon to hear people alternate between the languages (it reminds me a bit of what happens in French-speaking Canada). I have included another map in this chapter to help you visually reference and locate regional dialects.

If you listen closely to a person speaking, you may be able to tell where and how he or she grew up. Moreover, as in the United States, there are also regional dialects within each of the UK countries. In this chapter, I will highlight several English dialects as examples because that is the country I am most familiar with, and my ear is sensitive to the various accents I hear throughout England.

The English speakers in each English region and their respective cities have their own accents. You will even find differences within the larger cities. For example, in London you might expect to hear English being spoken in what is formally known as Received Pronunciation (RP) or the "Queens English", but East London is also known for its working-class cockney accent. You may be familiar with cockney rhyming slang – apples and pears (stairs), grief and strife (wife). In the

1980s, the term "Estuary" was given to the type of English accent that was being heard in the areas around the river Thames. The younger generation of Londoners combined elements of RP with cockney to create this unique estuary accent. There are areas of London and Bristol where the accent is heavily influenced by British Jamaicans. It is not uncommon to hear the phrase "Wagwan" (how are you?) or "Innit" (the slang or shortened version of "isn't it?"). When I was watching the television show *Top Boy,* I had to turn on the closed captions during some episodes because I simply could not understand what the characters were saying. I have found closed captioning a useful tool for when I am watching British television or films. Fortunately, when I am watching a Guy Ritchie film, Richard tends to be sitting right next to me and can translate. I think he has memorized most of the dialogue from Ritchie's film *Lock, Stock and Two Smoking Barrels.*

The Midlands, affectionately known as the "Heart of England", are divided into East and West regions. The historic counties of the East Midlands include Derbyshire, Leicestershire, Lincolnshire, Northamptonshire, Nottinghamshire, and Rutland. One of the more distinct accents heard in this area is the Derby dialect. Richard says folks in the Midlands sometimes refer to individuals as "duck" similar to when West Country folk use "love" (more about that later). A common local phrase, "*Ay up me duck*", can be heard throughout the region. Duck has nothing to do with waterfowl and instead is used as a term of endearment.

Herefordshire, Shropshire, Staffordshire, Warwickshire and Worcestershire comprise the West Midlands region. The West Midlands are known for having many of England's industrial cities, such as Birmingham, Leicester, Stoke-on-Trent and Wolverhampton. Today, the cities of Birmingham and Wolverhampton contribute to the largest polycentric urbanised areas (conurbation) in the Midlands. Despite being home to these large, industrial cities, there are parts of the Midlands that remain quite rural and agricultural.

To the North is beautiful Yorkshire. The Northern accent is the hardest for me to understand, and usually when I am up North, I ask for things to be repeated. However, I have been prone to give up when hearing accents from Northeast cities, such as Scarborough, Middlesbrough or Newcastle. It is then I have to rely on visual clues or just not engage in lengthy conversations. In the Northwest, you will hear the Scouse dialect when in Liverpool, and folks up that way are called "Scousers". The most famous Scousers were a popular little band from Liverpool called The Beatles! Although they are not that far apart, the Mancunian accent is easier for me. If you grew up in the Tyneside area, you would be a "Geordie" and speak with a Geordie accent.

As you move to the South West of England, in the areas of Gloucestershire, Wiltshire, Somerset, Bristol and Devon, you will hear the West Country accent. Once your ear becomes accustomed to the way words are pronounced, it becomes easier to listen to and understand what is being said. As a child, Richard's Bristol accent was quite broad, so his mother had him take allocution lessons in order to improve his speech. To this day, he stills remember one phrase from those lessons: "*how now, brown cow*".

In each region of the country, you will also find local patterns of speech and phrases unique to that area, such as in the prior example of the Derby phrase, "Ay up me duck!" In the West Country, the term is "luv", and the phrase is "You alright my luv?", although the "you" may or may not be pronounced. Everybody says it to everybody whether or not they know each other. It freaked me out when I first moved to Somerset. I had moved to the English countryside from Los Angeles, where you barely spoke to strangers, let alone refer to them as "my love".

For the most part, we (meaning Americans and Brits) speak the same language; however, there are a few everyday words that are used differently in the UK. The list below is not exhaustive, but it will help you begin to translate the more commonly used words.

English	American
Accommodations	Place to stay, either live (rent) or on vacation
Asian	Indian person (from Asia)
Athletics	Track & field
Bank holiday	Banks are closed, national holiday
Barrister	Lawyer
Bird	Young woman, slang
Biscuit	Cookie or cracker
Bloke	Man
Bloody	Expletive, general swearword
Bog paper or bog roll	Toilet paper
Braces	Suspenders
Bugger off	Go away/leave
Bum	Buttocks
Butty	Sandwich
Candy floss	Cotton candy
Car boot sale	Yard sale in a parking lot
Car park	Parking lot
Cash point	ATM
Casualty	Emergency room
Cheeky bugger	Smartass
Cheers or "ta"	Thank you
Chemist	Pharmacy, drug store
Cheque	Check
Chuffed	Happy
Cider	Alcoholic drink made from apples
Cinema	Movies
City Centre	Downtown
Cot	Baby's bed
Creche	Day care or nursery

Crisps	Potato chips
Diary	Calendar
Dinner (varies)	Lunch
Disembark	Deplane
Dole	Welfare
Dummy	Pacifier (for an infant)
Estate Agent	Real estate agent
Football	Soccer
Fortnightly	Every 2 weeks
Freephone	Toll-free phone
Fringe	Bangs (hair)
Frock	Woman's dress
GBP	Abbreviation for Great British Pound
GCSE or GCE Advanced Level	Abbreviation for General Certificate of Secondary Education or "O" Levels or "A" Levels
Gearbox	Transmission
Handbag	Purse
High Street	Main street
Hire	Rent (i.e., car)
Holiday	Vacation
Holiday	Vacation
Jumper	Sweater
Kit	Clothing or equipment
Knackered	Tired
Lad	Boy
Lay by	Rest stop
Lemonade	7-Up/Sprite type of soda
Lift	Elevator
Loo	Toilet
Lorrie	Truck

Manager	Coach
Mate	Friend
Mind the Gap	Watch your step
Motorway	Highway
Nan	Grandma
Nappies	Diapers
Pants (short for underpants)	Underwear
Pence	Penny
Piss Off	Go away
Pissed	Drunk
Pitch	Playing field
Plaits	Braids
Plaster	Band-Aid
Pong	Stinky
Poorly	To feel sick
Posh	Upscale
Post	Mail
Post Code	Zip code
Postbox	Mailbox
Pram	Baby carriage
Prawn	Shrimp
Presenter	Newscaster/TV Host
Primary School	Grade school
Pub	Bar
Public school	Independent, private school
Pudding	Dessert
Push chair	Stroller
Quaver	Eighth note
Queue	Line
Quid	£1, One pound sterling

RAC – Royal Automobile Club	Same as AAA
Redundancy/made redundant	Laid off work
Return (used when booking travel)	Round-trip
Ring road	The road/highway that goes around a city, typically
Roundabout	Traffic circle
Row	Argument
Rubber	Eraser
Rubbish	Trash
Ruck Sack	Backpack
Sacked	Fired
Scrumpy	Farmhouse, alcoholic cider
Seaside	Beach
Secondary school	Middle and high school
Sellotape	Scotch tape
Serviette	Napkin
Shag	To have sex
Silly cow	Silly woman (derogatory)
Snogging	Make out
Snooker	Pool type game
Sod's law	Something is inevitably irritating or has gone awry
Soil	Dirt
Solicitor	Lawyer
Spectacles	Glasses
Sponge	Cake
Straight away	Right now
Stone	Measurement of weight (I weigh about 7 stone or 100 pounds)

Supper	Dinner
Surgery	Doctor or dentist's office
Sweets	Candy
Swimming costume	Bathing suit
Take away	Carry out
The bonnet of the car	Hood
The boot of the car	Trunk
Till	Cash register
To 'ring' someone	To call someone
Toilet	Restroom
Torch	Flashlight
Trainers	Tennis shoes
Trolley	Shopping cart
Trousers	Pants
Tube	London underground, subway
Tuck shop	Snack shop
TV control	Remote
Underground	Subway
Waistcoat	Vest
Whinge	Whine
Yob	Hooligan
Zebra crossing	Cross walk

In addition to the aforementioned differences in terms, there are also slightly different pronunciations and spellings for some words. I have listed just a few examples of each:

Pronunciation differences:

Adidas – pronounced in English as - Odd-de-daz.
Garage – pronounced in English as – Gare-ah-ja
Schedule – Ch-ezdule

Mandatory – Man-date-tory
Innovative – Inn-na-va-tive
Aluminum (foil) – Al (like short for Alex)-la-mini-um

Spelling differences:

English	American
Apologize	Apologise
Tire	Tyre
Favorite	Favourite*
Color	Colour*
Check	Cheque

* It is common to see "or" have a "u" added to it in
English spelling.

The British Library has a recorded collection of British
voices and sounds that you may find interesting and helpful.
Once on the site, view by country – England – to hear the same
story from a variety of English-speaking voices. https://sounds.
bl.uk/Accents-and-dialects/Evolving-English-VoiceBank/

Unless your English man has spent a great deal of time
in the United States, he may also need some help translating
American slang. Here's a personal example. My maternal
side of the family is from the South, Tennessee to be exact.
When my relationship with Richard became serious, I decided
it was time for him to meet other family members. Richard
had not heard the Tennessee southern drawl (or twang), which
is quite distinctive, and on his first trip to Memphis I had to
translate. Richard and I were meeting my cousin Sigmund
on famous Beale Street. The first thing my cousin said to
Richard was "*What's up dog*?" He then asked if we wanted to
"*come by the crib and chill*" after he got off work. I told him
we were just passing through on our way to the "*ville*". He

said, "cool" and he'd "holla" at us later. After about five minutes of interacting with my cousin, Richard looked so distraught. I asked him what was wrong. He said he wasn't understanding much of what Sigmund was talking about, but he had heard Sigmund refer to him as a "dog". Not only does my cousin have a southern accent; he was speaking in Ebonics and using slang. Richard is now familiar with expressions such as "slow your roll", "YOLO", "beat down" (in reference to sport) and "bye Felicia!" I've caught myself saying "Well done darling!" or "good night Irene". I can't quite bring myself to say "alright me lover?" or "Richard's a gas head" (Bristol Rovers fan). However, I have said "that's proper lush" and "brizzle". I also have at my disposable several words to describe miserable weather – blustery, strong winds, chilly start, wet but mild, severe gales, breezy, unpleasant and high chance of rain, all of which can be delivered with a smile.

So, here's hoping this chapter has heighted your awareness of the language you might encounter while in England. When you're in the UK, you'll learn to speak English-English and when you are home in America, you might find yourself saying something that sounds slightly British, like "have a lovely day!"

CHAPTER 4

Food & Beverages

There was a time when British food was thought to be bland and boring. Times have changed, and British cuisine now ranks competitively among its well-known counterparts (the French and the Italians). In this chapter, we explore British food and beverages that a visitor or newcomer should include on the list of things to try whilst in the United Kingdom. You can find good food and drink throughout the UK from John O'Groats to Land's End, from the cities to country towns and small villages. You can dine in Michelin-starred restaurants, famous chef's restaurants or a 500-year-old pub. Your dining experience can vary from the "fry-up" at the local greasy spoon to the posh gastro pub, where you need reservations. There are pubs that serve good beer and cider and the food is a secondary thought or comes in the form of a bag of crisps. Locally sourced food and produce from the neighbourhood farm shop is also a good way to sample seasonal vegetables and fruits. Whether you are going for lake-to-plate or farm-to-table, go local and go fresh. My recommendation is to try them all!

Breakfast with Joe at The Chequers Inn, East Sussex

Food

In this section, I will help you recognise some typical British dishes you may find on the menu at the pub or in the local grocery store. I will also introduce you to some indigenous foods, such as haggis or glamorgan sausages. I think most Brits have a well-developed palate, eating everything from wood pigeon to Eton mess. However, there are some things my husband eats (i.e. Marmite) that I believe are an acquired taste.

When one thinks of British food, what immediately comes to mind? For most people, it is likely "fish & chips", right? This is a quintessential British favourite consumed by both nationals and tourists alike, but British food goes far beyond the local "chip shop". There are many dishes and foods that are unique to Great Britain. The local dishes and seasonal ingredients you can obtain are some of the best in the world. There is nothing like having a glass of local cider and a Ploughman's lunch in the village of Cheddar! In the next section, I describe a few of my favourite dishes and list some foods you may encounter or want to try whilst in the UK. The list is by no means exhaustive, but I have attempted to capture the wide variety of foods available and expose you to the rich British food heritage that should not go un-tasted!

My British favourites:

Full English Breakfast – This classic breakfast dish, or a variant of it, is served throughout the country and typically consists of: *back bacon rashers, pork sausages, ½ fried tomato, mushrooms, baked beans, fried egg, potatoes, black pudding and fried white toast cut in triangles with brown sauce, tomato ketchup and malt vinegar to accompany.* Sadly, I can never manage to eat everything on my plate. When they say "full", they mean it! This meal can also be called "the Full Monty", which is a reference to General Montgomery, who was known to eat a full English breakfast during WWII.

Bacon Sandwich or Bacon Bap – The English bacon is not like our bacon in America. These bacon sandwiches can be enough for breakfast on their own. *Back bacon rashers are nestled between a bap (bun) or slices of toast with plenty of butter.* I like adding brown sauce to mine – pure heaven! Richard suggests also adding English mustard for that special morning kick! (Zoe, our daughter, makes the best bacon sandwiches for us when we visit her, the toast has exactly the right amount of butter, and the bacon is not overly cooked.)

Cornish Pasty – This is one of my favourite quick bites for lunch. I am pretty traditional and like mine with beef, but it can be filled with lamb. It is made with a delicious crust and filled with *meat, diced potatoes and onions.* Pasties were often eaten by miners because they were easy to take and eat at work. My pasty was usually eaten with one hand whilst running to catch my train at Paddington.

Ploughman's Lunch – This consists of rusty bread or a baguette, a variety of cheeses, Branston pickle or some type of chutney, pickled onions, slices of cold meat and/or a slice of pork pie served on one big plate. As the name suggests, the dish has its origins as the ploughman's lunch. His wife may have thrown in an apple as well. I might start making this for Richard (minus the pork pie).

Roast Lamb with Mint Jelly and Lavender – This dish includes a delicious *rack of lamb, homemade mint jelly and a few sprigs of lavender, accompanied by roast potatoes, parsnips, carrots and peas.*

Roast Pork with Bramley Apple Sauce – I love pork chops, but roast pork with apple sauce and stuffing is something the British have perfected. It consists of *boneless leg of pork, onions, carrots, Bramley apples, brown sugar and butter.*

Rib of Beef with Yorkshire Pudding – This is, by far, one of my favourite dinner meals, probably because my husband does all the cooking. This is a traditional Sunday roast dinner which consists of: *Rib of beef on the bone roasted with onions and in beef stock, homemade Yorkshire puddings, candied carrots, perfectly roasted potatoes, cabbage or broccoli, gravy, horseradish sauce and traditional English mustard.*

Eton Mess – This is a favourite summer pudding of mine and consists of all things delicious – *strawberries, sugar, cream and meringues.* (The best I have had was served at the charming restaurant inside *Chequers Inn* in East Sussex.)

Meats & Meat Dishes

One of the unique shopping experiences I have in England is going to the butcher's for meat. I feel like I have stepped back in time. Sure, you can get meat at Sainsbury's or other supermarkets, but there is something special about going into the butcher shop and ordering your lamb chops and getting a bone for the dog. Please note that there may be slight regional variations for some of the meat dishes I have listed.

Back Bacon Rashers – English style bacon, similar to Canadian bacon in the U.S.

Bangers and Mash – sausages and mashed potatoes.

Beef Wellington – beef in a puff pastry.

Black Pudding – can also be referred to as "blood pudding". It is a type of sausage made from pork fat, onions, spices and pig's blood stuffed into sausage casing. It has a grainy texture and is black in colour, hence the name.

Cock-a-leekie – Scottish or Welsh beef stew with leeks.

Gammon – can be boiled after it is cooked. I call it ham.

Haggis – traditional Scottish food. It is a mixture of minced heart, lungs and liver of a sheep or calf combined with onions and oatmeal and boiled in the animal's stomach. People love it! Personally, I can't stomach it (pun intended)!

Lancashire Hot Pot – lamb (neck or chops), onions, potatoes, rosemary, salt and pepper, the meat is fried in a pan, the other ingredients are also fried and boiled. Finally, everything is layered in a casserole dish. The potatoes that have been thinly sliced are placed as the first layer, then alternating meat and potatoes, with the final layer being potatoes on top. The entire dish is covered and cooked in the oven.

Mince – meat that has been ground.

Poacher's Pie —usually attributed to the Welsh; this pie is made with beef, rabbit, chicken and game.

Pork Pie – this dish has been around for ages and is a British staple that is made of minced pork, onions, apple, seasoning, white wine and a little cognac, all in a pie pastry. It is served cold or at room temperature. It is a favourite in Northern England.

Salt Beef – In the U.S. we call it, "Corned Beef". I had to go to the butcher shop to get the brisket, as I could not always find it at the grocery store.

Sausages – vary in type and taste, most often in link shape, not patties. Sausage is frequently used to stuff turkey during the holidays.

Shepherd's Pie, Cottage Pie – beef minced meat, (you can also use lamb mince), onion, Worcestershire sauce, carrots, peas, diced tomatoes or tomato puree, red wine and mashed parsnips and potatoes for the top. All ingredients are mixed together, placed in a pie pan and cooked.

Steak and Kidney Pie - in England, this pie is filled with diced steak, beef kidneys and a thick beefy sauce.

Steak and Ale Pie – a variant of the dish above except with ale and no kidneys; Richard thinks the best beef and ale pie is served at *The Bull Inn* in Hinton, near Bristol. I like their Fish & Chips.

Streaky Bacon – Bacon as we know it in the U.S.

Toad-in-the-Hole – Yorkshire pudding with a sausage in it and gravy.

Poultry & Game Dishes

Duck with pancakes – can be found on the menu in most Chinese restaurants in England, the duck can be ordered either whole or half is served with parchment paper thin pancakes, hoisin sauce and cucumber. We think this dish it is absolutely addictive!

Game Pie – traditionally, a mix of game birds, rabbit and diced venison.

*Grouse – game bird

*Partridge – game bird

*Pheasant – game bird

*Pigeon (Wood) – game bird

Quail eggs – can be used to make delicious canapés

*Rabbit

*Venison

* Many of the game are seasonal foods. *Richard says watch out for the shooting pellets if you decide to shoot and cook yourself.* Otherwise, most pubs do a pretty good job of locally sourcing the game and offering delectable entrees. Again, I think *The Bull at Hinton*, in South Gloucestershire is a good example of a local village pub that serves good food, using local and fresh ingredients at a reasonable price. https://www.thebullathinton.co.uk/ There are places like this all over the country and the fun is in finding these gems!

Fruits

Most of the fruits we have in North America are available and known in United Kingdom, so many of the fruits you will recognize.

There are however, some fruits that are more commonly used in the UK depending upon the season. There are also some uniquely British dishes that call for certain fruits.

Apples – there are many varieties of English apples and they are distinguished by their function as eating, cooking or cider. Here are a few names you may see: Bramley, Cox, Pippin, James Grieve, Sunset, Russets, and my favourite, used for cooking, the Golden Noble.

 ***Berries*** - Blackberries, Elderberries, Gooseberries, Strawberries and Tayberries (best described as a bi-berry, it is a cross between a raspberry and a blackberry-see picture).The Tayberry was first cultivated in Scotland and is named after the River Tay. The Tayberry is typically available in the summer. They have a short season.

Currants - can be either red or black, they make excellent jams.

Sultanas - what we know in the U.S. as dried white grapes.

Fish & Seafood Dishes

Cockles – small shellfish, served raw or cooked. They are a traditional seaside snack. *Richard suggests that cockles eaten from a bag, covered in vinegar bought at the seaside are best.*

Cornish crab - found in beautiful Cornwall, I liken it to Maryland Crab cakes.

Dover Sole - white fish found off the coast of Dover.

Fish and Chips (French fries) – deep fried fish (i.e., haddock, plaice, skate, sole or cod) and thick cut potatoes also deep fried, typically served with mushy peas (green peas) and malt vinegar.

Fish Pie – a mixture of different fish (i.e., haddock, salmon, smoked cod) baked like a pie with a cheesy potato crust.

Herring – can be served pickled, salted or smoked.

Jellied Eels – chopped eel jellied in stock (Richard says this is a London favorite.)

Kippers – herring which can be served salted, smoked or pickled; Kippers in Milk-in Scotland, the herring is poached in milk

Smoked or Peppered Mackerel – I think these are self- explanatory.

Soused Mackerel – Mackerel cooked in vinegar.

Vegetables

As with the fruit, the same vegetables found in North America are also found in the UK The names may be slightly different, but the vegetable is the same. I have listed just a few.

Aubergine – In the U.S., we call it "eggplant".

Baked beans – are the same, however, in England, the beans are typically served on toast and eaten for breakfast.

Beetroot –beets can be roasted or pickled

Bubble & Squeak – Brussels sprouts, potatoes and cabbage mixed with bacon. Traditionally, it was made of leftovers from Sunday dinner. It can also have other cooked vegetables such as swedes or leeks in it.

Kale – the same leafy vegetable we have in the States.

Leeks – I found leeks to be used quite frequently in English dishes.

Parsnips – root vegetable, with sweet flavor, I like them roasted with a little honey.

Potatoes – there are quite a variety available in the UK King Edwards are a safe bet for an all-purpose potato.

Samphire – also known as sea asparagus can be found in the salt marshes around East Anglia during the summer, it can be steamed and served with butter.

Swede – root vegetable, you may know it as rutabaga.

Welsh Onion Cake – in Welsh, "teisen nionod", potatoes and onions layered with butter in a casserole dish and baked.

Cheese & Pickles

There is something to be said about having cheese in Cheddar! It is worth a drive to the West Country. You can stop by many local farm shops in addition to exploring the Cheddar caves and gorge. Many restaurants also offer a cheese plate with locally sourced cheeses. Pickles and Chutneys paired with the right cheese can be divine! I have listed a few of the common cheeses and pickles:

Cheddar

Double Gloucester

Red Leicester

Stilton (a type of blue cheese)

Branston Pickle – it is like a chunky brown relish with carrots, marrow (summer squash) mixed with vinegar, lemon juice, and various spices. Everything is cooked to until it is tender, yet crunchy. *Although it isn't pretty to look at, it is really, really good on crackers and sandwiches!*

Piccalilli – yellow pickled relish made from pickles, onions, cauliflower, vinegar and other spices. *I love it with ham.*

Pickled Beets, Eggs & Onions – *They like to pickle food in the UK.*

Ploughman's Lunch- *This dish can commonly be found on the pub menu.* It is a selection of cheeses, Branston pickle or chutney, pickled onions, gherkins, crusty bread, tomatoes, lettuce and may have a slice of pork pie or other meat (what is on offer varies from place to place).

Puddings (Desserts), Pastries and Cakes

Gooseberry Fool – is a chilled combination of gooseberries, sugar, dessert wine and cream. Other seasonal fruits like strawberries can also be used.

Burnt Cream – is the English version of crème brûlée.

Bramley pie –is an English apple pie.

Bread and Butter Pudding – I think this is similar to the Bread Pudding served in the States.

Christmas Pudding – traditional cake served at Christmas time, traditionally had a six pence somewhere hidden in it and whomever received was to have good luck (think of King Cake, minus the decoration and with fruit and alcohol).

Dundee cake – a version of fruit cake.

Eccles cakes – flaky pastry cakes filled with currants, sugar and sweet spices.

Hot Cross Buns – these buns are traditionally baked during the Easter season, best served warm and with butter.

Parkin – sticky cake made with treacle (syrup) sugar, butter, oatmeal, flour and ginger. This cake is served during Bonfire Night.

Rhubarb crumble – rhubarb pie with crumble on top.

Scones – served with tea, they may contain currants or raisins or served plain with jam or clotted cream.

Strawberries with Cornish Clotted Cream – strawberries served with a thick, delicious cream.

Shortbread biscuits – are shortbread cookies. "Biscuits" are cookies in the U.S.

Sussex pond pudding – sponge cake with a lemon in the middle for flavor.

Victoria sponge cake – named for Queen Victoria, it is sponge cake with jam or berries and cream in the middle.

Miscellaneous

Brown Sauce – a "brown" colored, tangy sauce, which I find particularly yummy on bacon sandwiches.

Chestnuts – a Christmas time favorite

Chutneys – There are a variety of chutneys available throughout the UK. I suggest you try at least one. *I am partial to the mango chutney, especially with an Indian dish.*

Colman's mustard – an English staple, can come pre-mixed or in powder form to mix yourself.

Coriander – also known as "Cilantro".

Elderflower jelly – Jell-O made with elderflower cordial.

Glamorgan Sausage — In Welsh, "Selsig Morgannwg," a dish consisting of cheese, bread, leeks and eggs, fried together in the shape of a sausage.

Icing Sugar – in the States, we call it "Confectioner's sugar".

Kentish cob nuts – these nuts are typically, available during the fall months.

Marmite – a yeast extract, brown paste-like substance, used on buttered toast, referred to as Marmite soldiers.

Scotch Egg – boiled egg rolled in breadcrumbs.

Treacle – sweet syrup used for desserts.

Watercress – green leaves and stems used for sandwiches and salads.

Welsh Rarebit - or "Welsh Rabbit" is cheese grilled on a slice of bread.

Sweets (Candy)

I consider candy, fun food! So, I decided to put it in the chapter. There are slight differences in the types of candy you find in Britain. Old-fashioned sweet shops still exist on some high streets in small towns or villages. I have included just a few sweets in this section. If you have a sweet tooth or children, you'll want to try something on the list.

Alphabet letters - Pink, orange, white and yellow hard, sugar candy shaped into letters of the alphabet.

Bassetts Licorice

Cadbury – Chocolate, chocolate, chocolate. This company has been around for ages and has worldwide recognition. Cadbury classics are enjoyed year-round, but the company is especially popular around Easter. They are known for making some of the best chocolate eggs in the world!

Flying saucers – these are round, disc-shaped candies, rice-coated with a sour filling in the middle (we don't have them in America).

Fruit salad – chewy mixture of fruit flavoured candy.

Mars – chocolate, chocolate, chocolate!

Maynards wine gums – gel-like candy, softer and sweeter than gummi bears. There is no "wine" in the candy.

Pontefract cakes – black, sweet, round liquorice with a stamp of Pontefract castle on the front.

Seaside Rock – traditionally found in seaside towns like Brighton. This sweet is a really sugary, hard rock candy. It comes in a variety of flavours. It can now be found all over, not just at the seaside, thank goodness!

Sherbet – a hard type of candy, fruit flavoured with a sherbet center.

Alphabet letters - pink, orange, white and yellow hard, sugar candy shaped into letters of the alphabet.

Cooking Conversions

When I am reading recipes and cooking in England, I need to make American conversions, to make it easier for me to understand. I've included a conversion guide you might find helpful to get you started.

Metric – American Measurement Conversions at a glance:

Liquids

Metric	American
150ml, ¼ pint*	⅔ cup
300ml, ½ pint	1¼ cups
450ml, ¾ pint	2 cups
900ml, 1½ pint	3 ¾ cups
1 litre	4 cups

Solid Weights

450g - flour	4 cups
450g - sugar	2 cups
450g - butter	2 cups (4 sticks)
450g - icing sugar	3 ½ cups confectioner's sugar
200g - rice	1 cup
100g – grated cheese	1 cup

Oven Cooking Temperatures (°C - °F)

110	225
120	250
140	275
150	300
160	325

Richard in the kitchen preparing Yorkshire pudding and roasted potatoes for Sunday dinner. Included in our kitchen staples are jars of *Piccalilli, Sharwood's Major Grey Mango Chutney, Lime Pickle, Colman's Mustard, HP Brown Sauce, Branston Pickle* and *Marmite.*

Beverages

In this section, I will briefly describe and discuss important British beverages, some you will recognize immediately and others you may need to read the description for clarity.

Tea

What is more quintessentially British than a cup of tea? Add to it scones and finger sandwiches and you are ready for the ultimate afternoon tea party! I only provide a brief history of this important beverage as it relates to the British, but you may find it interesting to investigate a full history of tea elsewhere.

In 1600, Queen Elizabeth I chartered the British East India Company, which became instrumental in trading spices, silks, cottons and tea. In the 17th century, Charles II married Catherine de Braganza of Portugal. Included in her massive dowry were tea and the seaports of Tangier and Bombay. Portuguese nobility were fond of drinking tea, the beverage du jour. Charles and Catharine drank tea, and if it was good enough for the "royals", it was good enough for everyone else in British society, although considered a luxury. Credit has been given to one of Queen Victoria's ladies-in-waiting, Anna Stanhope, Duchess of Bedford, as the first to hold afternoon tea parties. The Duchess is said to have started the tradition by requesting that sandwiches be brought along with her afternoon tea to her rooms in the Castle Belvoir. (During this time, there could be 7–8 hours between meals.) She began to invite her female friends over to partake in this late afternoon snack and for conversation. Once back in London, the Duchess continued her afternoon tea parties, and the practice began to spread throughout British society.

Coffeehouses gained popularity among men in the 18th century as places to go and have a drink and discuss the issues of the day. Women were not allowed in the coffee houses, but they could meet publicly in a tea garden if escorted by a male companion. Thus, afternoon tea parties also grew in popularity because women could be invited out to the homes of other women without being accompanied by a man.

High or Low Tea?

The distinction between high and low tea is often confused and has become blurred as a result of the confusion, or should I say "fusion", of the two (I have had low tea on a high table in a very posh establishment in Knightsbridge). Historically, "high" tea was more of a full meal. It is referred to as "high" because of the height of the table. A full dinner is served on a "high" dinner table. "Low" tea is a light meal or finger foods served in the late afternoon and ending before 7 PM. The height of the table is "low" (think American coffee table low) and was served in a drawing room or living room. In the classist British society, low tea was served to the upper class between lunch and dinner. Members of the working class would typically have "high" tea at the dinner table because it was their meal after working a full day. Richard often asks, "What do you want for tea Poppy?" Early on in our relationship, this used to confuse me, as I thought he was asking me what type of tea (Assam, Darjeeling, Lady Grey etc.) I wanted. Turns out, he was asking me what I wanted to eat for dinner! We have both learned to speak the other's language.

What is served during tea?

The menu for **Full Tea** includes tea (of course), savories, scones, sweets and dessert. The fare may consist of something like the following:

Sample Menu
for
Full Afternoon Tea

---

*West Country Cheddar Cheese Sandwiches with
Branston Pickle on Onion Bread*

---

*Cucumber Sandwiches with Cream Cheese and
Chives on Wheat Bread*

---

*Ham Sandwiches with Grainy Mustard on White
or Wheat Bread*

---

*Scottish Smoked Salmon with Caper Butter on
Rye Bread*

Egg Mayonnaise Sandwiches with Watercress

---

*Freshly Baked Scones with Cornish Clotted Cream
and Strawberry Preserve*

Assorted Tea Pastries and Cakes

Full Assortment of Black & Green Teas

On the menu for **Light Tea** is tea, scones and sweets.

What are the most popular types of teas offered during tea service?

Black Teas are favoured during tea service, with the most common being *Earl Grey*. The tea was named after the 2nd Earl Grey. It is a full-bodied black tea blended with orange oil of bergamot. *Lady Grey* is a milder variation of this popular tea and is made with lemon and orange. The other popular black teas typically originate from India or Sri Lanka (Ceylon).

English Breakfast is a combination of Indian and Ceylon teas.

Darjeeling is a floral, light tea.

Assam – named after the region where it is produced in India. Many of the breakfast teas are a blend of Assam (Irish breakfast, Scottish breakfast). It has a full-bodied, malty flavour and a strong, dark colour.

Green Teas are making a strong showing alongside the traditional black teas and are available as an option during tea service.

London Fog – Earl Grey tea, steamed milk and vanilla syrup.

Tea is traditionally served with milk, not cream. My family and I always add the milk after the tea has steeped. You can also request lemon with your tea, but do not combine milk and lemon, as the acidity in the lemon will cause the milk to curdle.

Beer, Cider, Gin and WHISKY

Ale is a barley-based malt.

Beer can be lager or bitter, with a taste varying from crisp and light to dark and strong. There are too many varieties of beer to mention. Here are some examples: Marston's Old Peculiar, Addnums Southwald Bitter, Flowers, Tinners, Guinness (Irish), Brains and Bishop's Tipple. *Richard's personal favourite is Wadsworth 6x.*

Cider is traditionally made from fermented apples or pears. Cider can range from sweet to dry. My favourite is **The Orchard Pig** apple cider made in Somerset. I also order a ½ pint of **Scrumpy Jack's** when in a pub.

Gin – there are so many, Plymouth, Gordon's etc., but I like Bombay Sapphire because of the bottle.

Stout is a dark beer made from barley and roasted malts.

Whisky – without the "e" is the English spelling. Malt, blended, Scottish, and Irish are a few varieties of the many varieties to choose from when in the UK. *Penderyn* is a Welsh whisky that has been made since the 19th century. *The English Whisky Co.* is a 21st century newcomer to whisky distilleries. Names like Dewars, Glenlivet, Clan MacGregor, Glenfiddich, The Macallan, Bells, Bushmills are pretty well known. There are many more whiskies produced in the British Isles, so if you like whisky, it is worth a trip to a distillery to try and find a favourite.

Other Beverages

Apple Brandy – made with apples and popular in Somerset.

Baby Cham – not to be confused with the Jamaican dancehall artist, this is an alcoholic sparking perry, popular in the 1960's and 70's, which was marketed to women. I like the little fawn that the company uses as its logo. It is not so popular these days, but I like it!

Cadbury drinking chocolate – this is hot chocolate UK style.

Horlicks Malt Drink – I do not know how to describe this drink… it is made with malt and wheat, ground to a powder, to which you add milk and enjoy.

Lemonade – this is a fizzy lemon drink, more like 7-Up or Sprite, not the U.S. lemonade.

Pimm's – a dark liqueur first produced in the 1800's by James Pimm. It makes a delightful summer drink or cocktail with fresh fruit and lemonade. Nothing says summertime in England like Pimm's.

Ribena – I like the black currant concentrate that you mix with water. It also comes pre-mixed in a variety of flavours.

Robinsons Orange Squash – this drink tastes like squashed oranges.

Snowball – Advocat and lemonade (the English lemonade) garnished with a cherry!

Wines – there are varieties from all over the world in every price range.

Let's just say, you will not be thirsty in the UK. There are plenty of beverages to quench your thirst. I am partial to tea. I think many Brits are, despite there being a *Starbucks* or *Costa* Coffee in almost every city in England.

CHAPTER 5

Sports, Religion & Politics

I have always liked watching sports: indoor, outdoor, winter, summer; it doesn't matter. I didn't play that many when I was young. I was not tall enough for basketball and could never get the hang of field hockey. I played lacrosse for one year in high school and took up squash in college to get some exercise. My dad taught me how to roller-skate (is that a sport?), and because we lived in Michigan, ice-skating and sledding were favourite wintertime activities. Growing up, my mom had season tickets to the Detroit Lions; it was our "girl-time" activity. I would attend an occasional Pistons' basketball game, and if the Red Wings were in the playoffs, I would watch on television. Detroit boxers were legendary and important to the city, as evidenced by the placement downtown of the Joe Louis boxing arm and fist by sculptor Robert Graham. My father did a little boxing when he was young, and I remember watching heavyweight title fights with him. Detroit was a great sports town.

However, I had never witnessed true passion for sport until I met Richard. I realised the powerful effects of sports when I utilised a soccer metaphor after we had an argument. I don't even remember what we were arguing about, but I knew I had heard enough. I went to my craft box (I was into scrapbooking at the time) and cut some red construction paper into a rectangle. I handed the small sheet of paper to Richard. Yes, I took him straight to a "red" card. For those of you who understand, this was the worst possible outcome for Richard. In soccer, a red card is given for a severe infraction. When a player receives a red card from the referee, he or she is ejected from the game and the team is down a player. It is given for a serious offence, and by showing Richard a red card, he knew the quarrel was over. The effect was immediate: the arguing stopped; he was in a state of shock for about five minutes. He just sat there shaking his head. I know he was saying to himself: "No, she didn't just give me a red card!" It was from this point that I begin to carry a yellow and red card in the glove compartment of the car (just in case). We had only been dating a few months when this incident occurred, but I learned how to use a sports analogy to shut down an argument quickly.

If you date an Englishman, you must be prepared to share him with the sport (or sports) he chooses to love. Don't try to compete, because, when it's all done and dusted, you will end up losing. Instead, introduce him to American sports, such as baseball. He will already know terms like, "up-to-bat", "catcher", "umpire" and "outfield" from playing or watching cricket. I'll explain more about the sport of cricket a little later in the chapter.

In terms of American sports, the National Football League first made its way to England in 2007 and has since established a yearly presence in London. Typically, two NFL teams play a regular season game in England, with one team being the "home" team. I am not sure how it is decided which teams play, but it is exciting to know that American football is being played in England! The UK NFL fan base has grown, and it is entirely likely that your Englishman may already be familiar with American football and teams. Major League Baseball has also made its way to England and this favourite American pastime is anticipated to garner a respectable following of fans each year. The English like their sport. As I mentioned earlier, they are some of the most fervent, zealous and ardent sports fans in the world. Each sport in this chapter has been the focus of numerous books, so be forewarned that I am only providing a "taster" of these areas as I cannot cover each of them in-depth in a single chapter. I am only going to mention a few of the sports you need to know so that you will not feel completely at a loss when he is with his mates and the discussion of (*insert sport name*) comes up.

Occasionally, you might hear the terms "Home Nations" or "Home Countries" used in sporting circles. Often these terms refer to the countries of the United Kingdom – *England, Wales, Scotland* and *Northern Ireland* – as a collective. If the reference is specific to Irish rugby or cricket, the term Home Nations expands to include the entire island of *Ireland.* The terms may also be used in the sport of British cycling to refer to the countries of the United Kingdom and the Isles of Jersey, Man and Guernsey (also known as the Crown Dependencies).

Remember, this is just a "taster" list and not exhaustive, so if your loved one's sport is not on the list, apologies. You must also be forewarned that I will not list the complete rules and equipment for each sport or go into detail of how the game is played or the event actualised. Think of this chapter as a reference list; if you want to learn more, go to the sport's official website. I will start with the most recognised sport in the world and continue with sports or sporting events you might come across in England.

1. Football

Whatever you do, do not say: "Oh, you mean soccer." Instead you might say: "Oh yes, the beautiful game!" You will immediately earn a feather in your cap for that remark. To give you some insight and to help with understanding the mindset of the football fan, here is a quote from Bill Shankly, one of the most beloved managers of Liverpool Football Club:

"*Some people believe football is a matter of life and death, I am very disappointed with that attitude. I can assure you it is much, much more important than that.*"

The English play football at various levels, from professional to amateur. There are youth leagues, reserve leagues, nonleague clubs, county football associations, five-a-side weekend pub clubs and the English Football League, but the big daddy of them all is the English Premier League, or simply the Premier League. The name of the league is a bit of a misnomer because in addition to local lads, the English Premier League teams attract football talent from all over the world. Brazilians, Welsh, Scottish, Spanish, French, Italians, Dutch and even a few Americans have played in the English Premier League.

The season is from August to May. In the current structure there are 20 teams in the Premier League. The top teams stay at the top and play in championship games, and the lowest placed teams each season are relegated to the English Football League. The games are typically scheduled on Saturdays and Sundays. There are a few teams that have dominated over the years and are consistently at the top of the league: Liverpool, Manchester United, Arsenal, Chelsea, Tottenham Hotspur and Manchester City. Hopefully you have heard of at least one of these clubs! At the time of writing this book, London is the city with the most teams in the Premier League: Arsenal, Chelsea, Tottenham, Fulham, West Ham United and Crystal Palace. Teams can lose their place in the Premier League if they have a losing season. Each year, three teams are relegated. Teams can avoid relegation by winning.

In addition to the Premier League games, there are other important events in English football culture that you should know: the UEFA Championship, the FA Cup and the FIFA World Cup (which only takes place every four years). The Union of European Football Associations (UEFA) sponsors the annual competition among the top European football teams. The UEFA Championship final is a true sporting spectacle and English teams have typically performed well in this competition. The Football Association (FA) is the oldest football association in the world, having been formed in the mid-1800s. The Football Association's Challenge Cup competition, as it is officially known, is one of the most exciting domestic cup challenges around. The FA Cup is so exciting because it is a competition in which league and non-league teams play their way to Wembley Stadium in London, each having an equal chance of winning.

The Fédération Internationale de Football Association (FIFA) is the organisation responsible for sponsoring major international football tournaments, in particular the World Cup. The FIFA World Cup brings together the international community for one of football's biggest spectacles. England has won the World Cup once, and whenever they make the finals, you will hear the phrase "football's coming home" touted by the English fans. The national jerseys/kit (uniforms) change, but you can be assured that the "three lions" will be represented.

 The men's national team jerseys have a lone gold st*ar, indicating one World Cup win. I am hopeful that in my lifetime, I will see another star added to the national team's jersey. An important note about the jerseys: players either wear their "Home" kit or the "Away" kit depending on where they are playing. The jersey colours for the national team are typically a combination of red, white and blue.

Quick reference – the game basics of football:

- Two teams run up and down a field (also called a "pitch"), passing a ball and trying to score a goal without using their hands. The pitch is at least 100 yards long with goalie boxes at each end. There are 11 players on each team – 1 goalie and 10 field players.
- There are 2 periods of 45 minutes each, with a 15-minute halftime break.
- The very basic skills involved in football are dribbling, running, passing, heading, shielding and changing direction. In a game, you may see corner kicks, penalty kicks, free kicks and missed kicks.

Player Roles:

Defenders: These players try to stop the opposing team from scoring. They play in front of the goalkeeper. The central defenders play in the middle of the field, and the defenders on the left and right flanks are called "fullbacks".

Forwards: These players are supposed to score goals or create opportunities for others to score.

Midfielders: I call these players transitional. They go forward when on the attack and take defensive positions when the opposing team has the ball.

Goalie or Keeper: This is arguably the most important player on the team. The goalie's job is to keep the ball out of the net and prevent the opposing team from scoring. The goalie is the only player allowed to use his hands. *There have been American keepers that were good enough to play in the English Premier League. I am partial to Brad Friedel and Tim Howard, but Kasey Keller, Brad Guzman and Marcus Hahnemann also did us proud on the international stage. I would be remiss if I didn't* *mention Karen Bardsley, the California-born goalie who played for Manchester City Women's Football Club.*

Need-to-Know-Football Vocabulary:

Football Boots: What we call cleats.

Free Kick: Can be indirect or direct and is given to a team as a result of an official offence by the opposing team.

Home & Away Kit: The uniforms that players wear during home games are different from those worn when visiting another team. Uniforms will also change if the opposing team has the same team colours.

Match: The term used to describe two teams playing against each other.

Offside: A player is considered offside if any part of the body (including head and feet) is in the opposing team's half and nearer to the opponent's goal line than the second-last opponent and the ball. (A visual probably explains this better; I suggest watching a game.)

Penalty Kick: These kicks are typically taken when a player commits a free kick offence inside the penalty area.

Pitch: This is the playing field.

Red or Yellow Cards: Both are bad. A yellow card is given to a player (or players) by the referee as a warning. Two yellows and "you're out" of the game. A red card also means you are automatically disqualified or, as the English say, "sent off" from the game for committing some serious offence. A player who receives a straight red card is also suspended from playing in a minimum of three games. I have also heard Richard refer to a player receiving either colour card as being "booked". I think this is in reference to the referee writing the offence down in a little notebook. A red card booking is detrimental to the team because the booked player cannot be replaced, leaving the team a player short for the remainder of the match.

Referee: The referee enforces the rules of the game during the match and keeps time and notes. The referee is assisted by match officials, including the video assistant referee (VAR).

Stoppage or Injury Time: These terms refer to extra minutes added to either period because of loss of time due to player injury, substitutions, wasting time or any other delay to play determined by the referee. Typically, stoppage time is anywhere from one to eight minutes, but its length is at the discretion of the referee.

Win, Lose or Draw: In football, a team can win, lose or draw a game. The objective of course is to win, but you can tie, which is better than losing.

For more detailed information on the rules (laws) of the game, visit the Football Association's website.

My Advice: For those women who do not follow soccer, if you are dating an Englishman, you should start. Even if he does not have a favourite premiership team (which I am sure he does), he most likely follows his hometown club or the national team.

2. Cricket

A very brief history of cricket seems appropriate as it is overshadowed by other sports in America but is a favourite sport of the English (and of the populations of former English colonies across the globe). Cricket is probably the sport in this chapter that many Americans know the least about, which is why I have taken the liberty to write considerably more about it than the other sports I have included in the chapter. If baseball is America's national pastime sport, cricket is England's. I remember when Richard first explained cricket to me, my eyes glazed over and the words he was speaking went in one ear and out the other, until he said: "And then they break for tea." That's when I regained my attention. I can't think of another sport that purposefully stops for tea and lunch! So, not only do cricketers have the best-looking traditional uniforms (cricket whites) and play in warm and beautiful parts of the world, they break to eat and drink; how could I not come to love this quintessentially British game? In my head, the closest analogy I can think of is being at the ballpark, watching the Cincinnati Reds and eating a hot dog and having a cold beer. So, in my mind, to understand cricket, I referenced baseball terms that were similar, such as, umpire, pitch, innings, ball, field and bat. Eventually, as I became more comfortable with the sport, I stopped referencing baseball and just opened my mind to learning about cricket.

According to the International Cricket Council, the origins of the game date back to Norman or Saxon children playing in the south-east region of England. In the 17th and 18th centuries, cricket developed from a children's game into an adult sport. Women were also developing their cricket talents during this time and the first recorded women's match took place in 1745 in Surrey. The Laws of Cricket were first written in 1744. The Laws have been in the custody of the Marylebone Cricket Club (MCC) at Lord's since 1787, and MCC was, and still is, responsible for any revisions.

During the 17th century, English colonists brought cricket to North America. The English colonists also took the game with them to the Caribbean, Australia and India in the 18th century. The sport began to be played in South Africa and New Zealand during the early part of the 19th century. Interestingly, the first international cricket game was the USA versus Canada, played at St. George's Cricket Club in New York in 1844.

Today, there are national cricket teams in England, Scotland, Wales and Ireland, but only England play in what are called the "Tests" matches. The Tests represent the highest level of professional cricket games. Welsh, Scottish and Irish players are eligible to play for England. Test matches last up to five days, with each team having two opportunities to bat. The all-important Test series between England and Australia is known as "*the Ashes*". This name is a reference to the ashes of a wooden bail that are apparently inside the winning urn. It's an urn, but it's also a trophy. I just go with the winning symbolism and don't over think it.

The governing body of cricket in England is the England and Wales Cricket Board, abbreviated to ECB. The board's home is at Lord's cricket ground in London. England is a full member of the International Cricket Council (ICC), which oversees the global governance of cricket. The ICC

Quick Reference - the game basics of Cricket

- The team consists of 11 players. Players can be batsmen, bowlers, wicket keepers and fielders.
- The pitch (field of play) size can vary but is usually circular or oval in shape. In the centre of the pitch you will find the **wicket** (described in the vocabulary section). The edge of the field is known as the boundary edge and represents whether you're in play or out.
- Traditionally matches at all levels are supervised on the field by two umpires. The umpires stand at each wicket and count the number of overs (also explained in the vocabulary section). Bowlers must deliver 6 legal bowls to equal an over.
- At the start of the match, the captains of the teams decide whether their team will bat or field by tossing a coin. The first batting team tries to score as many runs as possible in the given time. The teams then

change positions: the batting team becomes the fielding team and vice versa. The second batting team tries to outnumber the runs scored by their opponents. The team with the most runs wins!

Players and Roles:

Richard considers Sir Ian Botham the greatest cricket player he's seen in his lifetime. I'm partial to Sir Alastair Cook; it's probably a generational thing. I know in part that Richard's affinity for Botham is because he started his cricketing career in our beloved first-class county of Somerset. Cricket, as a sport, is indebted to W.G. Grace, one of the first great cricket players in England. Grace is responsible for increasing the popularity of the sport across the country during its development in the 19th century. Having seen photographs of W.G. Grace, what strikes me is his long, full beard; it was quite an unexpected image. It also speaks to how trends come and go and come back again. He would fit in with many of today's modern athletes who 'sport' a beard.

The following are cricket team player roles:

Batsman: This player tries to hit the cricket ball and defend his wicket. He uses the cricket bat (flat-fronted and made of wood) to hit the ball. It is a batman's job to defend the wicket and not let a bowler hit it.

Bowler: The bowler "bowls" or, as I use to erroneously say, "throws" the ball in an attempt to hit the stumps the batsman is trying to defend. My cricket-loving Englishman did try to explain to me that a bowler can be a "fast", "slow", "swing" or "spin" bowler, depending on the technique the player uses when bowling. Bowlers who are also good batsmen are called "all-rounders".

Non-striker: This is the batsman positioned at the bowling end of the pitch, not hitting the ball.

Wicketkeeper: This is the player located behind the stumps or the wicket. The wicketkeeper can either "stump" the batsman out, catch the ball or run out a batsman if need be. You can easily recognise the wicketkeeper in a game because of the squatting stance taken during a bowl (looks similar to the umpire position in baseball).

Allow me a quick digression, Richard is from a family of miners on his maternal side. There were coal pits located all over Bristol, one being in an area called Warmley. This is where Richard's family has lived for generations. In 1908, his great-grandfather, Henry Ettle, died mysteriously in the local mine shaft. His death was tragic because he was relatively young when he died (around 40) and his wife was left to raise Richard's grandmother (the baby in the photograph) and her 5 siblings on her own. I write about this family connection here, because the inquest into Henry's death was conducted at the King Billy (the pub near Richard's childhood home) by the local Coroner, Dr. Edwin Mills Grace, the brother of W.G. Grace, the bearded cricket player, I mentioned earlier.

Need-to-Know Cricket Vocabulary

Ball: The cricket ball is red for test matches and white for one-day games. It is usually made of cork.

Bails: These are wooden sticks placed horizontally on top of the stumps to form the wicket. Bails determine when the wicket is broken, which determines when a batsman is out.

Bouncer: This is a type of ball bowling technique used by a bowler. As indicated by the name, the ball bounces and hopefully does not injure the batsman.

Bye: This occurs when no player touches the ball, but the 2 batsmen run anyway.

Googly: This was a cricket word long before the search engine we know as *Google* was invented. It is a type of spin-bowler ball delivery technique.

Home of Cricket: This refers to Lord's Cricket Ground in London. It is probably the most famous cricket ground in the world. I have heard that it is also one of the best places to watch a game. Lord's is home to the Marylebone Cricket Club Museum, which is dedicated to cricketing art and memorabilia. A day out at Lord's is sure to be a memorable experience, as you can bring a picnic, pre-order a hamper and enjoy the lunch break.

Leg Before Wicket (LBW): This is when the ball hits any part of the batsmen's pads or body, thereby impeding the ball striking the wicket.

Over: Six bowls delivered to a batsman constitute 1 over. Once six bowls are delivered, the umpire calls "over" and another bowler is selected to bowl from the opposite end of the pitch.

Run: A run occurs when a batsman hits the ball and the two batsmen at the wicket are able to complete their run to the other side of the pitch. Runs can also be scored if there is no ball, a wide ball, a bye or leg bye.

Stumps: These are three vertical pieces of wood that form the wicket. The two pieces of wood that lay on top of the stumps are called bails.

Wicket: This is defined as a small gate. In cricket there are two sets of three stumps, 22 yards apart. The wickets are located at either end of the pitch.

To learn more about cricket, visit the Lord's website and the International Cricket Council's website.

A reader note: I am forsaking the details of other sports mentioned in this chapter because more likely than not, you are already familiar with most of them. So, forgive the simple descriptions. I must leave you to research the specifics. Therefore, for the remainder of the sports, I will only list the name of the sport and possibly the major sporting event associated with it that takes place in England (or the UK). There is no particular order to the sports listed. Also, please don't be offended if you don't see a sport that you play or know of not listed. It's just a sample list.

3. Rugby Football

In the simplest of descriptions, I liken rugby to American football without the pads and helmets. One team has the ball and the other team tries to stop them from scoring by tackling players. The players run from one end of the field to the other, passing, throwing or kicking the ball. The goal is to get the ball into the end zone to score points. The team with the most points at the end of the game wins. I hope the purists forgive me for lumping both kinds of rugby football together in the title. To be clear, there is *Rugby Union* (15 players comprise the team) and there is *Rugby League* (13 players make up the team). They have separate governing bodies and slightly different rules. To learn more about Rugby League, visit the International Rugby League website. To find out more information regarding Rugby Union, visit the World Rugby website.

4. Tennis

Wimbledon is the oldest tennis tournament in the world and is played on grass. It is held at the All England Lawn Tennis and Croquet Club.

5. Equestrian Sports

Horse racing – A few of the well-known races are:

- *Royal Ascot*
- *Cheltenham Festival*
- *Grand National*
- *The Derby (Epsom)*
- **English horse riding** – dressage, jumping, eventing
- **Polo** – This is a team sport played on horseback. Players use a mallet to strike a small hard ball through the opposing team's goal. Think field hockey on horseback. Personally, I think the uniforms are almost as good-looking as cricket whites. To learn more about polo go to the Federation of International Polo website.

6. Golf

This sport really belongs to Scotland and the *Open Championship* is the only major golf tournament held outside of the United States.

7. Bowls

Historically, a form of bowls can be traced to 13th century England. It reminds me of the Italian game Boccia, where players roll (bowl) balls. In England, I see people playing it in the park. Did you know there are bowling greens in Central Park in New York City?

8. Squash

Squash is a racket sport that reminds me of racquet ball but with a smaller racquet. (It is also a term used for certain flavoured drinks that can be mixed with water.) Squash apparently originated in 18th century London prisons, but in the mid-19th century it was modified by boys at Harrow School in London. I learned to play it in college and have enjoyed it ever since.

9. Snooker

This is a billiard game. The championships are always on television in England. It looks like pool with the same shaped table, different coloured balls and a cue stick. If you can play pool, you'll probably be able to play snooker.

10. Darts

Yes, darts is a sport. One can be a professional dart player and belong to either the Professional Darts Corporation or the British Darts Organisation. This is another sport where its championships are always on television in England. It's also played in the pub.

11. Water Sports

There are so many water sports and off the top of my head, I can't think of any that differ from what we have in America. Is fly-fishing considered a sport?

12. Rowing

These are 2 well-known races:

- *The University Boat Race* (Cambridge and Oxford)
- *Henley Regatta*

13. Athletics

This is what we in America call track & field sports – sprint races, hurdles, long-jump, discus throwing.

14. Winter Sports

The same winter sports we enjoy in America are played and enjoyed in England.

15. Motor-car racing

I should have probably listed the larger category of **motorsport**, but I've only paid attention to car racing because of Lewis Hamilton and Jenson Button.

British Grand Prix

16. Fell Running

I suppose this is a sport, maybe a hobby, but it is something I had not heard of until living in England. It is similar to trail running and popular in the part of England known as the Lake District.

17. Ballooning

There is nothing like seeing hot air balloons in flight on a clear day in Bristol during the *International Balloon Fiesta*.

Religion & Politics

I could write volumes on religion and politics in England, but that's not the purpose of this book, so I am going to keep these sections short (really short). I once heard a funny story that fits with this section of the chapter on religion. I was told if you ask an Englishman if he goes to church on Sunday and he answers "yes", you need to clarify which church - the football pitch or the building used for religious worship. Pele once remarked that football was like a religion to him and I think many English fans can be compared to religious zealots. There are houses of worship (stadiums), prophets (managers), angels and demons (players). I think you get the analogy. So, for this reason, you may want to re-read the section at the beginning of this chapter on football. Suffice it to say, Henry VIII broke away from the Catholic church in the 16th century and established the Church of England. The Archbishop of Canterbury is the senior leader of the church, but the reigning monarch is considered the head of the church. Although the majority of people in the country are Anglican, England is home to many different religions and spiritual practices. If you take a citizenship test, you will need to know this fact.

For politics, what is important to know is that England is a constitutional monarchy. We have a "ruling" monarch and a prime minster. In conjunction with individuals either in the *House of Lords* or *House of Commons*, they make political decisions on behalf of the British people. At the time of my writing this book, the UK was leaving the European Union, in a move appropriately titled "Brexit".

My Advice: Chances are you have already been given the advice to not talk about religion or politics on your first date. I agree with this advice, if you are just starting your relationship with an Englishman, leave religion and politics for later. Instead, talk about your favourite sports! Enjoy getting to know him as a person. His views and values will surface in due time.

CHAPTER 6

Holidays, Music & British Cultural Identifiers

I have divided this chapter into three parts. Part I provides a sampling of important English (or British) cultural holidays. Part II briefly discusses the importance of music in British culture and how British musicians have global influence. Part III offers a random list of unique cultural identifiers you may find interesting, including the British Broadcasting Corporation (BBC).

——————————— PART I ———————————

Holidays

In England, as in the United States, many holidays and celebratory days commemorate important figures or events in the nation's history. National holidays are often referred to as "bank" holidays because the banks and most businesses are closed on these days. Generally, employers give their employees these days off work. There are eight bank or public holidays in England:

New Year's Day: 1 January

Good Friday: March or April

Easter Monday: March or April

Early May Bank Holiday: May

Spring Bank Holiday: May

Summer Bank Holiday: August

Christmas Day: 25 December

Boxing Day: 26 December

In America, we have national holidays similar to the aforementioned English ones, except Good Friday, Easter Monday or Boxing Day (the day after Christmas) are not considered national public holidays. As the name indicates, Easter Monday takes place the day after Easter Sunday. It makes for a 4-day short break when combined with Good Friday. Boxing Day occurs on the 26th of December. There are two theories surrounding its origins. The first idea comes from the Christmas boxes the wealthy would give to their household servants who had to work on Christmas. Servants would have the day off to celebrate with their families. The second theory refers to the alms collection boxes that were in the church during advent. Church clergy would distribute the collection among the poor on December 26, the feast of Saint Stephen. Saint Stephen was known for his acts of charity and work with the poor. In modern times, Boxing Day has become a day for watching sport and relaxing.

There are other cultural holidays in the yearly calendar that are also important in England:

Mothering Sunday or Mother's Day always comes earlier than Mother's Day in the United States; it is 3 weeks before Easter Sunday.

Father's Day is the 3rd Sunday in June (the same as in the U.S.).

Remembrance Day is always observed at the eleventh hour on November 11th. This references when World War I ended in 1918. Remembrance Day pays homage to all the service men and women who lost their lives in war, serving their country. Red poppies, symbolising Flanders' Fields and the lives lost during WWI, are sold for charity, and worn in the several weeks leading up to the day. On Remembrance Sunday, which is the second Sunday in November, a member of the Royal family typically lays a wreath at the Cenotaph in London. It is a very sombre occasion.

St. George's Day occurs on the 23rd of April. St. George is the patron saint of England. Northern Ireland, Scotland and Wales also have patron saints – St. Patrick, St. Andrew and St. David, respectively. Only Northern Ireland and Scotland have their respective patron saint's day as an official holiday.

Valentine's Day is celebrated on February 14, as it is in the U.S. Galentine's Day (February 13) is currently not celebrated as much, but I suspect it will gain traction in the UK and become an unofficial celebration of female friendship and women celebrating women, as it is the U.S.

Halloween has grown in popularity and commercially since I moved to England. For my first Halloween in England (in the early 2000s), I bought bags of candy and had a big bowl by the door. No one came to trick or treat, not one child. I cried; it took me ages to eat all that candy!

Bonfire Night, also known as Guy Fawkes Night, is celebrated on the 5th of November with fireworks, bonfires, food and festive drinks. It marks the failed attempt of Guy Fawkes and other Catholics involved in the 1605 Gunpowder Plot to blow up parliament and kill King James I. "Remember, remember the

5th of November" is the rhyme children learn to introduce the holiday. I was slightly taken aback by this celebration, not only because I am Catholic, but also because it entails a man (Guy Fawkes) hanging in effigy over a bonfire, and this reminded me a bit of lynching and southern clansman burning crosses.

The reigning monarch's birthday is typically celebrated with a parade, but it is not considered a public holiday.

PART II

Music

The fact that I have dedicated an entire section to music shows its significance in the United Kingdom. In England, there is an enormous appreciation for all types of music, and British musicians have influenced and continue to impact the music we listen to and enjoy. In actuality, this could have been a chapter on its own. I have had to limit my discussion in the crossover section to naming only a few bands and singers, when there are so many more I wanted to mention. So, apologies to those British musicians (i.e., Kanneh-Masons), songwriters (i.e., Sam Smith), DJs (i.e., Mark Ronson) and record producers (i.e., George Martin) that I did not include in the chapter. I also confess that there is a heavy bias and focus on "pop" music, rock and roll bands, and R & B musicians of a certain era. There is less attention given to the many great British classical and jazz musicians who have filled the airways with their sounds, and for that I am sorry; their contributions are very much appreciated. I wrote many pages of this book listening to the UK's *Scala* radio and *JazzFM*.

There is an interesting cultural identifier related to music in England that happens during the Christmas holiday season. It is the revealing of the Christmas number one song. I debated whether I should put this topic in the music section or the cultural identifier section since it applies to both, but I decided it made more sense to put it here. The Christmas number one song is decided by sales during the week leading up to Christmas Day and holds the top spot on the UK Singles Chart. When I first moved to England, I found it quite curious that such a big deal was made about a song but having lived in the country for over 10 years, I now too have gotten caught up in the excitement. The bookies take bets and families make bets on which song will be number 1. Sometimes the song has a Christmas theme and sometimes it does not; it really depends upon public sentiment. The UK Singles Chart officially began in 1952. Here is a representative list of artists/singles that have been named "Christmas #1s" over the years:

- 1957 Harry Belafonte – "Mary's Boy Child"
- 1958 Conway Twitty – "It's Only Make Believe"
- 1963 The Beatles – "I Want to Hold Your Hand"
- 1964 The Beatles – "I Feel Fine"
- 1965 The Beatles – "Day Tripper/We Can Work It Out"
- 1966 Tom Jones – "Green, Green Grass of Home"
- 1967 The Beatles – "Hello, Goodbye"
- 1972 Jimmy Osmond – "Long Haired Lover from Liverpool"
- 1973 Slade – "Merry Xmas Everybody"
- 1974 Mud – "Lonely This Christmas"
- 1975 Queen – "Bohemian Rhapsody"
- 1976 Johnny Mathis – "When a Child Is Born" (Soleado)
- 1979 Pink Floyd – "Another Brick in the Wall" (Part 2)
- 1981 The Human League – "Don't You Want Me?"
- 1984 Band Aid – "Do They Know It's Christmas?"
- 1987 Pet Shop Boys – "Always on My Mind"
- 1988 Cliff Richard – "Mistletoe and Wine"
- 1989 Band Aid II – "Do They Know It's Christmas?"
- 1990 Cliff Richard – "Saviour's Day"
- 1991 Queen – "Bohemian Rhapsody/These Are the Days of Our Lives"
- 1992 Whitney Houston – "I Will Always Love You"
- 1995 Michael Jackson – "Earth Song"
- 1996 Spice Girls – "2 Become 1"
- 1997 Spice Girls – "Too Much"
- 1998 Spice Girls – "Goodbye"

- 1999 Westlife – "I Have a Dream / Seasons in the Sun"
- 2000 Bob the Builder – "Can We Fix It?"
- 2001 Robbie Williams and Nicole Kidman – "Somethin' Stupid"
- 2002 Girls Aloud – "Sound of the Underground"
- 2003 Michael Andrews and Gary Jules – "Mad World"
- 2004 Band Aid 20 – "Do They Know It's Christmas?"
- 2006 Leona Lewis – "A Moment Like This"
- 2007 Leon Jackson – "When You Believe"
- 2008 Alexandra Burke – "Hallelujah"
- 2009 Rage Against the Machine – "Killing in the Name"
- 2011 Military Wives with Gareth Malone – "Wherever You Are"
- 2012 The Justice Collective – "He Ain't Heavy, He's My Brother"
- 2013 Sam Bailey – "Skyscraper"
- 2015 Lewisham and Greenwich NHS Choir – "A Bridge over You"
- 2016 Clean Bandit ft. Sean Paul and Anne-Marie – "Rockabye"
- 2017 Ed Sheeran – "Perfect"
- 2018 LadBaby – "We Built This City"
- 2019 LadBaby – "I Love Sausage Rolls"

What you will notice about the Christmas #1s list is that there are several repeat artists and songs (The Beatles, Cliff Richard, The Spice Girls, LadBaby, "Bohemian Rhapsody", "Do They Know It's Christmas?") that claim the number one spot in different years. You will also note that many American artists have made the Christmas #1 chart. What I have come to love about the Christmas number one is that it can be an old song, a new song, a silly song or a song for charity that touches people from all walks of life because by the time Christmas rolls around, almost everyone in the country will have heard it.

Music Crossover

Music is an important part of my life and it very much contributed to my relationship with Richard. Remember my email pseudonym was "Sunshine Hendrix"? Well, I later found out that Richard loved, loved, loved Jimi Hendrix. Perhaps he was thinking I might have been related, although he never indicated any disappointment when I revealed I was not. On our first dinner date, I took Richard to the Third Street Promenade in Santa Monica. The restaurant was playing Jimi Hendrix, which we considered a fortuitously good sign for our budding relationship. Little did we know then that the music of Jimi Hendrix would continue to play an important role in our lives. On that first date, we talked about how music was such an important part of both of our childhoods and growing up. We discussed how my Uncle Bobby was a member of the original Drifters and sang lead on the song "Drip Drop", and how my mother played piano for her church choir when she first moved to Detroit. I told him I was a volunteer violin teacher with a programme in Watts called "Sweet Strings". The programme gave children in South Central L.A. the opportunity to learn to play a stringed instrument. Lessons were taught on the weekends by community volunteers and instruments were donated and given to the children to take home to practice. He told me of his love for the English composer Elgar in particular, Nimrod and the "Pomp and Circumstance March No. 1" (The Land of Hope and Glory). As many times as I had heard this march at graduations, I never knew the composer was English. It is quite a spectacle to see this played during *The Proms* series in the Royal Albert Hall in London.

Richard told me the first album his Dad bought was Nat King Cole.

Thinking about this as an adult, Richard found it amazing that in the late 1950s an Englishman from Bristol loved listening to a Black American singer. He recalled his first Led Zepplin concert and seeing Ginger Baker play with his band in a barn in the early days of Glastonbury. I told him that when I was a junior varsity cheerleader, we would cheer Queen's lyrics, "we will, we will rock you!", and how at championship games people would start singing "we are the champions".

He knew of America's love for The Beatles, John Lennon and Paul McCartney as solo artists, and the Rolling Stones, but he hadn't realised how big Clapton or Pink Floyd had been in America. What struck me was how much musical crossover there was (is) between America and England. Many English musicians acknowledge the influence of Black American musicians on their playing and sound. Jimi Hendrix moved to London in the mid-1960s and died there when he was only 27 years old. In that short time, he influenced so many great guitarists, both British and American. I had forgotten that The Police was a mixed group and that Stewart Copeland, the drummer, was American.

I was a teenager in the 1980s when there was another British music invasion; bands like Flock of Seagulls, Bronski Beat, Depeche Mode, Thompson Twins, Spandau Ballet, Dexy's Midnight Runners, The Human League and so many others had hits on the American music charts. I told Richard my high-school years were filled with music. I explained that in American high schools, it was typical to have an annual musical and my first high-school performance was singing a solo in the play *Godspell* junior year. My senior year, I had been selected to play Dorothy in *The Wiz*, but for some reason we couldn't get the rights and my drama career came to a disappointing end. Personally, I think the headmistress was hesitant about performing a Black musical at a predominately White, all-girls, Catholic high school. So, in addition to playing classical violin and listening to Motown artists, gospel, R&B, jazz, disco and house music, I listened to Phil Collins, Dire Straits, John Lennon, Culture Club, Rod Stewart, The Police, Adam Ant, Billy Idol, Wham, the Pet Shop Boys and David Bowie. Later, in college, it was Peter Gabriel, Simply Red, George Michael, Alison Moyet, UB40, U2, the Eurythmics, Elton John, Elvis

Costello, Duran Duran and Sade. Tears for Fears dominated our college bar and during primal scream (the one-time during exam prep, everyone on campus could release their study anxiety, by yelling out the window) their song "Shout" blasted out of my dorm window. After college, it was Soul II Soul, Maxi Priest, Dido, Seal and Lisa Stansfield. One of my favourite duets is Lisa Stansfield with Barry White, singing her song "All Around The World". I also admitted to liking a few Spice Girls songs. Later when I moved to England, I fell in love with the music of British female artists, such as Joan Armatrading; her Radio 2 Piano Room rendition of the "Weakness In Me" is another of my top listening/viewing musical choices. My list of favourite British female artists includes, Corrine Bailey Rae, Amy Winehouse, Duffy, Adele, Alison Balsom, Alison Moyet, Jorja Smith, Annie Lennox and Joss Stone.

It was as an adult that I remember my parents playing Lulu after watching the Sidney Poitier movie *To Sir With Love* or my father in the basement playing "Hey Jude" by The Beatles. I fondly remember watching the Tom Jones show on television with my mother and her thinking he was so handsome. At the time, I didn't know he was Welsh. I'm not sure my mom knew or cared; she just loved his curly hair. My concert going days slowed down in my 30s, but Richard and I did manage to take in a few during our time in Los Angeles – Eric Clapton, Alisha Keys at the Hollywood Bowl and Sting. Richard came to a Sweet Strings recital at the University of California Los Angeles. (I think he had started to fall for me, why else would he put up with screeching sounds coming from little violinists?) In Cincinnati, we enjoyed "Uncle" Charlie Wilson, Bootsy Collins, the Isley Brothers, John Legend, John Mayer, Alison Balsom (she was playing in Indianapolis) and watching Gareth Malone on television as he worked his magic with school choirs. We were part of a faithful group of English fans who enjoyed hearing the Rolling Stones play in Paris. In Wales, we heard the indefatigable Shirley Bassey. On the Bath Rugby pitch, we listened to the young Jamie Cullum. In

London, we watched and listened to the genius that was Prince. I saw the legendary Buena Vista Social Club at The Royal Opera House in Convent Garden. We enjoyed Elton John playing at Longleat as part of the Safari Park's 50th anniversary celebrations. Although we both have our favourite genres, we like being introduced to new music that has come out of our respective countries. For instance, at the time Richard moved to Los Angeles (early 2000s), I was listening to a lot of Pharrell Williams, the Neptunes, Gwen Stefani, No Doubt, The Black Eyed Peas, The Red Hot Chili Peppers, Snoop Dog and Dr. Dre. These musicians I considered "local", as I was living in Venice, California at the time.

Since I had moved from the East Coast to California, I brought with me late 80's, early 1990's East Coast Rappers, New Jack Swingers, Hip-Hop and R & B artists such as, Jay-Z, Teddy Riley, Chubb Rock, Slick Rick, DJ Jazzy Jeff and the Fresh Prince, De La Soul, Mary J Blige, Jill Scott, The Roots and A Tribe Called Quest. Of course, I could never forget where I came from and my Midwest roots, so wherever I went, the Minneapolis sound of Jimmy Jam & Terry Lewis, the Queen of Soul, Aretha Franklin, trumpeter, Donald Byrd, Motown legends Stevie Wonder and Marvin Gaye were always carried with me. Thankfully, he had heard of Herbie Hancock, The Commodores and Earth, Wind & Fire. He knew about one famous Tina, the seemingly ageless, Tina Turner and learned from me about the other, soulful Tina Marie. He appreciated these introductions and in subsequent years recognised songs by these artists when I would play them.

Richard reminded me that before Phil Collins went solo, he was a member of Genesis. He had the entire CD collection of early Genesis, which I had never heard. He introduced me to Jools Holland as an individual artist; I had fallen in love with Squeeze in college but had not realised that Holland had been a band member until my conversation with Richard. He had a special place in his heart for Portishead and Massive Attack. Richard loved Ska and Reggae. As a young teenager, he would listen to Desmond Dekkar and Prince Buster. I had never heard of either of them. So, I let him listen to Jimmy Cliff, Third World and Lauryn Hill. Of course, we both loved Bob Marley. Sometimes, for date night, we would simply pull out CDs and reminisce about our younger days. Richard would put on The Beatles, Madness, The Pogues, Take That or Robbie Williams. He made me listen to Pink Floyd and Oasis, and I gained a new appreciation for their music. He learned from me about the incredible acapella group Take 6, Gloria Estefan, Meshell Ndegeocello, Eminem and Queen Naiji (my homies from Detroit). He bought me Tupac and 50 cent CDs. We would listen to Carlos Santana, I particularly loved the song "*Maria, Maria*" (my middle name is Maria). It is no surprise we chose a guitarist to play at our wedding. As we drove through the Southern regions of the U.S., he came to understand the disturbing meaning of Billie Holiday's song, "Strange Fruit". In New Orleans, he heard and tried two-stepping to Zydeco. How can anyone not want to dance when you hear that distinctive accordion and washboard sound? He listened to my varied musical taste that included artists such as, Arrested Development, Andre Watts, Ella Fitzgerald, Maxwell, Missy Elliott, Wynton Marsalis, Brian Culbertson, Leidsi, Etta James, Michael Franks, Luther Vandross, Itzhak Perlman and Yo-Yo Ma. I even introduced Richard to a few British artists – Soul II Soul, Paul Hardcastle, Stereophonics, Jamiroquai, Ed Sheeran and Coldplay. We both hold a special place in our hearts for James Brown, Michael Jackson and Whitney Houston. Our love of music has been an integral part of our relationship. Sometimes when we have an argument, we cool down by watching music videos, or a music documentary, and the anger dissipates. Our time in Nashville, gave us more of an appreciation for country music. Although Richard had always listened to Johnny Cash, we started listening to country artists such as Carrie Underwood, Little Big Town and Florida Georgia Line. I'm not sure if Taylor Swift considers herself a country singer anymore, but we have been known to listen to Ms. Swift. I like country rap and am particularly drawn to the Lil Nas X remix of "Old Town Road" with Billy Ray Cyrus. More Southern rock than country is how I would classify Alabama Shakes. There is something so mesmerizing about lead singer, Brittany Howard, her voice, her guitar playing, her gesticulations, her glasses! I feel the music when she sings. I love her solo work even more than Shakes, perhaps because the songs are so personal.

One Christmas, Richard gave me a Mumford and Sons CD because I love their song "I Will Wait", and he remarked: "You know their British right?" I had to admit, I did not. "It's okay Poppy", he would say with a smile. Often times, singers lose their accents when they perform, and you would never know they were from the UK until you hear them speak. Now, my ear is trained, and I can on occasion recognise a British singer. For instance, when I listen to my favourite 80s Britpop songs or bands, I hear the accent in certain words. "I Melt With You" is a song by Modern English with catchy lyrics, and when they sing the word "better", it comes out as "bet – ah", which is the English pronunciation.

We had the television programme *Later.... with Jools Holland* to thank for keeping us up-to-date and introducing us to musicians such as Chase & Status, Disclosure and Clean Bandits. I adopted the Clean Bandit and Jess Glynne songs, "Rather Be" and "Real Love" as the songs of our romance. The lyrics, the violin and the fact that I can dance to these songs were perfect musical representations of my relationship with Richard. Despite both of us being older now, we still surprise each other with recommendations of young British and American artists. For instance, Richard introduced me to Ariana Grande, and I introduced him to the British grime artist Stormzy, cellist Sheku Kanneh-Mason and songwriter and pianist Reuben James. He also respects the music of Minneapolis native José James and the American jazz singer Gregory Porter whose song "Real Good Hands" could have easily been Richard's message to my parents when we were dating.

Music Festivals

As I stated in the beginning of this section, music is an important feature of British life. Music festivals are popular events attended by old and young alike. Many of the festivals attract not only international musicians but have a global audience, particularly if the festival is televised or streamed live. It's surprising to me that the outdoor music events are so popular because British weather is so mercurial. However, many of the festival tents are not like the tents I had when I went camping; they are rain-proof and much more luxurious and glamorous. I think for British youth, attending a music festival is a rite of passage. It's hard to compare the British summer music scene to anything in America. I suppose the closest comparisons are Coachella, SXSW, Lollapalooza, The New Orleans Jazz & Heritage Festival, The Newport Jazz Festival, Bonnaroo and the Columbus Jazz and Rib Festival (which I have to mention given my paternal roots in the city of Columbus). I only mention a few UK festivals in this section, but I encourage you to find one that fits with your musical taste. There are so many British music events taking place in the summer that every weekend can be filled with a musical festival of some sort. I am going to start the list with one of the most well-known and beloved music festivals: Glastonbury.

Glastonbury – This is the big daddy of the summer music festivals. Known worldwide, it features musicians from every genre, as well as current and old-school artists. It usually has something for everybody. Get out your wellies and camping gear; it takes place in Pilton (my neck of the woods) in June. It always sells out.

Isle of Wight – If Glastonbury is the daddy, IOW is the granddad of British musical festivals, having been on the scene for more than 50 years. It takes place mid-June. The line-up varies year-to-year but always features a nice mix of dance, rock and pop music. If only I had been around to see Jimi play the Isle of Wight!

BoomTown – As the name suggests, this is a bass-driven music festival usually featuring a roots and reggae musical line-up. It takes place annually in August in Winchester, England.

Reading & Leeds – These festivals take place in late August in the cities of Reading and Leeds. These festivals started as primarily rock band festivals but have grown and diversified to include a mix of indie bands, dance and hip-hop artists.

Latitude – This is more than a music festival; it is a woodland adventure. Set in Suffolk in mid-July, the festival is family friendly with music, comedy acts all set in the natural beauty of Henham Park. It sells out early.

The Proms – Classical music enthusiasts also enjoy 8 weeks of music, family friendly activities and music-oriented workshops in London. The first and last nights of the Proms are spectacular and worth watching on television or attending in person. The Proms started in the summer of 1895 and have been presented ever since. The name has been shortened from the words "Promenade concert". Originally, the concerts were held outdoors in London's pleasure gardens and people were free to stroll the gardens as they listened to music. In the 19th century, indoor proms increased in popularity and Sir Henry Wood began as the Proms first conductor. The Proms is sponsored and hosted by the BBC (discussed later in the chapter).

—————————— PART III ——————————

Random British Cultural Identifiers & the BBC

This section lists a few of the distinct cultural identifiers and iconic features or figures that will be familiar to your Englishman. Most of this list will have been a part of his cultural upbringing and if you date (or marry) him, you will come to know the features on this list too, if you don't already. Again, I must make a disclaimer and say this is not an exhaustive list, but one that has more personal significance than generalisability. The list is random and in no particular order; it starts with what came to mind first when I was writing.

1. The local (or village) pub and the pub quiz
2. Buckingham Palace Guards with (American) bearskin caps
3. Sir Winston Churchill
4. Heathrow Airport
5. The BBC*
6. Charles Dickens, Andrew Lloyd Webber, Julian Fellowes
7. Fish and chips shop, high street curry house
8. Harry Potter and James Bond characters
9. Remembrance Day, poppies and the Spitfire
10. Print versions of The Times (especially The Sunday Times), The Daily Telegraph, The Guardian, The Daily Mail
11. Shakespeare and the Globe Theatre
12. Jane Austen – *Pride and Prejudice, Sense and Sensibility, Persuasion, Emma, Mansfield Park* and *Northanger Abbey*
13. London neighbourhoods, buildings and landmarks – Big Ben, Houses of Parliament, Buckingham Palace, The Tower Bridge, Soho, Westminster Abbey, London Paddington

Station, Notting Hill, The Gherkin, St. Paul's Cathedral, Covent Garden, Brixton, Baker Street, Marylebone, Oxford Street, Canary Wharf, Fleet Street, Sloane Square, The Docklands, Tate Modern, The West End

14. Victoria sponge cake and Cadbury Chocolate
15. Sir David Attenborough, Dame Judy Dench, Stephen Hawking, the 1966 England World Cup championship football team
16. Foodies (people or tv associated with food) – The Great British Bake Off, MasterChef, Jamie Oliver, Lorriane Pascale, Marco Pierre White, Merry Berry, Gary Rhodes, Ainsley Harriott, Jason Atherton, Nigella Lawson and Gordon Ramsay
17. Bletchley Park and Alan Turing
18. The Brontë Sisters (19th century novelists and poets from the Yorkshire area of England)
19. Charlotte Brontë – *Jane Eyre*
20. Emily Brontë – *Wuthering Heights*
21. Anne Brontë – the youngest and probably the lesser known of the Brontë sisters – *The Tenant of Wildfell Hall*
22.
23. The Most Excellent Order of the British Empire honours
24. London Fashion Week & Crufts, "Best in Show"
25. The Rupert Annual, The Dandy Annual
26. Seaside towns – Blackpool, Weymouth, St. Agnes, Brighton
27. The Royal Horticultural Society – Chelsea Flower Show
28. Christmas pantomimes and January sales
29. Political or royal scandals – just pick a decade and there will be one or the other (or both)
30. English Heritage and National Trust sites – places throughout the UK known for historical significance or natural beauty
31. The Mini-Cooper and Bentley
32. David Austin Roses, Allotments and public footpaths

33. David John Moore Cornwell – a novelist known by the pen name John le Carré; author of *Tinker, Tailor, Soldier, Spy* and many other spy novels
34. Snooker, bowls and darts televised championship games
35. The Queen's (or King's) speech
36. Electric lawn mowers, country and agricultural shows – Royal Bath & West, Doe, Tendring
37. White Cliffs of Dover
38. Half-term holidays
39. Abbey Road Studios
40. Television programmes (some current – others available to purchase or stream):
    - *Downton Abbey*
    - *Dr. Who*
    - *Strictly Come Dancing*
    - *Blue Peter*
    - *Match of the Day*
    - *University Challenge*
    - *Prime Suspect (with Dame Helen Mirren)*
    - *Eurovision*
    - *Question Time*
    - *Countdown*
    - *Time Team*
    - *Later….with Jools Holland*
    - *Faulty Towers*
    - *Soap Operas – EastEnders, Emmerdale, Coronation Street, Hollyoaks, Casualty*
    - *Dad's Army*
    - *Little Britain*
    - *Blackadder*
    - *Top Gear*
    - *Gavin & Stacy*
    - *The Office*
    - *The South Bank Show*
    - *The Voice*
    - *Have I Got News for You*

- *Britain's Got Talent*
- *Top of the Pops*
- *Desert Island Discs (radio programme)*
- *X-Factor*
- *Monty Python's Flying Circus*
- *Countryfile*
- *Grand Designs*
- *The Great British Bake Off (both adult and junior)*

41. Banksy – Bristol artist
42. The gastropub

I started the list with "the pub" and I am ending the list with "the gastropub"; it's only fitting, as there is nothing quite like a great English pub (or gastropub).

* Number 5 on the list of cultural identifiers is the British Broadcasting Corporation (BBC). A special point regarding this institution has to be made, as my Englishman calls it "the state propaganda machine". The BBC is a public broadcasting service and is the oldest public broadcasting service in existence. It is also one of the largest due to its many subsidiaries, which include BBC News, BBC Weather, BBC Radio, BBC Films and BBC Music. Richard remembers that when he was growing up there was no other choice in radio or television. The BBC controlled the airways, the corporation controlled what people saw and heard, hence his moniker the "state propaganda machine". I occasionally watch the BBC Breakfast team in the morning. The BBC has also reached American shores. It has become a worldwide British cultural export. When we are in America, I often catch Richard watching BBC World News America (with our favourite presenter – Katty Kay) in between his recorded premier league football games. There are other channels for choice now,

but it is not hard for me to imagine the dominance the BBC had (and to some extent still has) in England. As I mentioned at the start of the book, England and Great Britain have such a rich and long history, it is impossible to include everything. This chapter was an attempt to give you a little insight into some of the cultural influences that may shape the worldview and perspective of your partner. It is also a personal list, as much of what I have experienced and learned about British culture is through the lens of my Englishman.

CHAPTER 7

Daily Living & the Necessities

The reality of living in England is that despite the fact they speak English, it is still a foreign country. My adjustment to living in England took about a year. Actually, taking up residence was completely different from being on holiday and visiting for a few weeks. It was difficult leaving sunny California and becoming acclimatized to the grey, overcast weather. I also had trouble understanding the broad Bristol accents and people from up north. At least when I went "up north" back home (Michigan), I could still understand what people were saying to me. In England, it was not like that at all. There were many times in the beginning of my life in England that I would just smile, nod my head and carry on. I kept thinking, things are so similar and yet, so different. I began to question, am I really going to be able to live here? Was my fairy-tale dream becoming a nightmare? I then thought of all the American women who had come before me and mustered up strength to keep calm and carry on. Surely, I could do the same.

In an effort to lessen your anxiety, I'll start this chapter on daily living and necessities with things that were important to me right away when I arrived in England. Remember the adage I mentioned in the beginning of Chapter 2? Well, I am using it again here but with my added modifications. The exciting part of living or travelling in England and around the UK is that *where you are will determine what you see, what you do, what you hear, what you eat and maybe even what you wear*! As an expat, knowing some very basic information about daily life in England will make your transition to British life easier. This chapter has been written to provide you with the very basics you will need to survive. I have organized it by category so that you can quickly reference a topic of interest. These areas of daily living are only a starting a point; you must find what works for you, your lifestyle and your relationship.

Money & Banking

Money...Money makes the world go around...the world go around...the world go around. A mark, a yen, a buck or a pound...a buck or a pound...a buck or a pound...is all that makes the world go around.

"MONEY" SONG LYRICS FROM *CABARET*
PERFORMED BY JOEL GREY & LIZA MINNELLI

 The English currency is known as the British pound (GBP). The pound sterling, simply referred to as "the pound", uses the currency symbol £. They don't use shillings anymore, although you will hear them referred to in movies and books. The following notes (bill denominations) most commonly used are the following:

£5 - The five-pound note, also known colloquially as a "fiver".

£10 -The ten-pound note, also known as a "tenner".

£20 -The twenty-pound note.

£50 – The fifty-pound note.

There are also pound coins: a one-pound coin (topmost coins in the picture) and a slightly larger two-pound coin (underneath the pound coins). The one-pence coin (penny) is equivalent to our penny. Rather than saying, "pence" you will often hear the change referred to as "pee"; so, two pence becomes "2p" or fifty pence becomes "50p". There are 1p, 2p, 5p, 10p, 20p and 50p coins.

Money is easy to calculate as one hundred pence is equal to one pound. The exchange rate is always variable. Sometimes, the pound is strong against the dollar, and other times, it works in reverse. Bureaux de change locations where you can convert your dollars to pounds can be found in airports, some larger department stores, banks, posts offices and train stations. Remember, you are typically charged service and commission fees, so it is a good idea to shop around for the best price.

Credit cards, such as Mastercard and Visa, are widely accepted in England and throughout the UK. Most cards use a chip and pin for purchases. American Express and Diners cards are not as frequently accepted as the aforementioned credit cards.

Banks in England operate in much the same way as they do in America. Depending on the type of account you want to open, you might need a letter of introduction, identity documents or proof of employment and proof of address to open your UK bank account. English banks use sort codes instead of routing numbers. You also spell "checks" as "cheques". Most chequing accounts, typically referred to as "current accounts", come with an automatic overdraft (which has saved me on multiple occasions). You will not find notaries or safe deposit boxes at the bank though. You can set up direct deposits and pay bills or people with relative ease as long as you have the sort code and account number. Normally, it only takes a few hours, if not minutes, for money to reach another person's account if they hold a UK bank account too. I have found that getting US dollars through your bank is cheaper than using a bureau de change. The bank gives you the current exchange rate, which is competitive, without charging commission rates. You can also use your UK debit card to withdraw money from most automatic teller machines (ATM) when you are in America. The ATM is called a "Cash Point" in the UK, and it works the same way as an ATM, with its primary function being to dispense money. What you don't see much of is drive-through banking. In fact, drive-through businesses in the UK are pretty much contained to the food-service industry.

My Advice: To be honest, this is partially my mom's advice. My mom (who was a completely modern, independent, and empowering woman) always told me to "have your own", meaning, have your own interests, ideas, thoughts and MONEY! She particularly emphasized the money part. So, relatedly, I think it is a good idea to hold onto your own U.S. bank account and make sure there is enough money in it for a flight to America, just in case you need to get home for an emergency. If you are planning to relocate to England, open an account with a bank that has an international service, which means you can find a branch whether you are at home in the States or in England. I also recommend Internet banking to help you keep track of your money, no matter where you are in the world. I have one bank that allows me to have an account in England as well as an account in the U.S. I am also able to transfer money between accounts, which has come in handy and saves dealing with wiring services and fees.

Shopping – Food

Grocery Stores — There are major stand-alone grocery stores (i.e., Waitrose, Morrisons), and then there are grocery stores that are part of a larger retailer (i.e., Marks and Spencer). Some larger grocery stores will carry more than just food; you can shop for clothes and home products too. Whole Foods Market, a name you are most likely familiar with, is making its way into the UK food retail business. Most of its locations are in the London area. Selfridges, on Oxford Street, also has a food shop where you can find American brands and specialty foods. So, whenever I have a hankering for foods from home, I go to Selfridges and stock up. However, more and more British stores are stocking many American brands, and thanks to the Internet, you can always order online. (I ordered bags of Cheetos Puffs online because I could not find those anywhere.) Here are the names of several food stores (in addition to those I have mentioned above) you will find in England. I have also included convenience shops, which are much smaller but have the essentials if you just need to pick up something quickly.

- Tesco
- Asda
- Sainsbury's
- Aldi
- Lidl
- Iceland
- SPAR (convenience)
- Tesco Express (convenience)
- Londis (convenience)
- Co-op
- Costcutter

I am able to find some American food items in Asda and Tesco. Most of the major grocers also offer online shopping and home delivery service.

Specialty Food Shops — In England, they still have specialty food shops (which I love), such as butchers and fishmongers. Just a reminder that in some places, the butcher may have to order your corned beef (or salt beef, as they say in England). You may also find shops dedicated to selling just fresh fruit and vegetables. We are also fortunate to have several local farm shops in the area. Even if you are in the city, you can find locally stocked farm-to-table shops that offer seasonal groceries and kitchen staples.

Embarrassment Saver — If you are shopping at the grocery store, don't wait for someone to pack your groceries. I made this mistake when I first moved to England. Thank goodness, Richard was with me. He politely whispered, "We pack our own bags here." Unlike in the States, having bag packers and someone to help you out to your car is not the norm in England. For the most part, you will have to pack your own bags. Occasionally, the person working the till (the cash register) may offer to help, but more often than not, you are on your own. Also, be sure to bring recycled bags for your groceries; otherwise, you will be charged a few pence per bag by the store. Some stores also charge a pound to rent a shopping cart. You'll get the pound coin back when you return the cart.

Shopping — Clothing

Shopping for clothes in England is much the same as it is in the States. You can shop for men's, women's and children's apparel, shoes and accessories at designer shops, bespoke clothiers, department stores, vintage-clothing boutiques and charity shops. The larger retailers that can be found in most major cities in England are

- Marks and Spencer
- John Lewis (yes, like the U.S. Congressman from Georgia)
- Harvey Nichols
- House of Fraser

They even have T J Maxx, but it is called *T K Maxx*. In London, you will find the iconic *Harrods*, which is unlike any place I have ever shopped. I can't even describe the "Harrods experience", for me it is sensory overload. There are floors dedicated solely to women's clothing. There is the food level, there is a restaurant for when you tire of shopping and want to eat. You could spend an entire day in the store. Suffice it to say, I only go to Harrods now if folks who come to visit me from America request it.

In most of the major cities in England, there are shopping areas, not all of which are in the city centre. So, it is worth getting out to explore whichever city you are near. I would like to mention a few shops that are my personal favourites: In London, there is *Liberty*. I love the name, but in addition to that, the store is unlike any other, with its Tudor outer façade and cosy inside rooms and unique accessories. *Selfridges*, on Oxford Street, is another favourite department store of mine not only because of its American history, but the flagship London store's window displays are legendary. *Fortnum and Mason*, another landmark store that has been in existence since the early 18th century, has what I think are some of the best gift hampers in England. London has great shopping in various parts of the city, not just on Oxford or Bond Streets. For example, on Marylebone High Street, you will find not only trendy and designer clothing shops, but opticians, homeware shops, one of the best independent bookstores, *Daunt*, and my favourite mom and children's boutique, *Rachel Riley*. If you happen to be in any of my favourite cities to the west, I recommend visiting the Clifton area of Bristol. Clifton Village has a variety of independent retailers with locally sourced items from jewellery to vintage clothing. In Bath, you can find Jolly's (House of Fraser) and most known apparel shops on Milsom Street, but I like going down the less traversed side streets to find truly unique clothing boutiques and accessory shops.

- **Outerwear:** The UK climate dictates that you invest in various types of outerwear: boots, hats, coats, jackets and scarves. Thank goodness, the range of outerwear clothing is vast, both in terms of style and cost. If you are going to the English countryside, dress appropriately! (The country life is what I know best, since I only lived as a London city girl for about nine months.) In the country, your wellies are your best friend. Wellington boots come in all different colours and patterns. The boots are named after the first Duke of Wellington. Although the design has been changed and modified, his name remains associated with boots (and beef). I have a traditional Hunter pair in that fabulous drab, olive-green, and when I want beautiful style, I choose from my selection of Joules boots. I have found that cashmere, flannel, moleskin, wool and cotton make the weather more tolerable. I recommend having at least one pair of wellies and one waxed cotton jacket in your closet. Here are just a few companies that are known for either durable, stylish (or both) outwear Mackintosh and clothing:

Welligogs
Barbour
Aquascutum
Boden
Joules
Lavenham
Ness
Private White, V.C.
Hunter

There are so many wonderful British clothing companies that I have not listed. Have fun shopping for your outerwear. You'll be surprised how you'll find yourself wanting to take walks in the rain!

Clothing & Shoes – Size Conversion Charts

The charts below compare US, UK and European sizes. Oftentimes, you will find European sizing as well as UK sizes listed in English clothing shops, so I have included both on the charts below. These charts are only guides, and although the clothing manufacturer may have indicated a certain size on the label, sizes may differ considerably between English designers and shoemakers and their European counterparts.

Women – Clothing size conversion

US	0	2	4	6	8	10	12	14	16	18	20
UK	4	6	8	*8/10	*10/12	14	16	18	20	22	24
European	32	34	36	38	40	42	44	46	48	50	52

* I have found the sizing can really depend on the clothes and whether you like to wear them loose or snug.

Women – Shoe size conversion

US	4	5	5.5	6	6.5	7	7.5	8	8.5	9	9.5
UK	2	3	3	4	4	5	5	6	6	7	7
European	35	36	36	37	37	38	38	39	39	40	41

Men – Conversion chart for men's suits, coats and jackets

US	30	32	34	36	38	40	42	44	46
UK	30	32	34	36	38	40	42	44	46
European	40	42	44	46	48	50	52	54	56

Men – Conversion chart for men's dress shirts (based on neck size)

US	14	14.5	15	15.5	16	16.5	17	17.5	18
English	14	14.5	15	15.5	16	16.5	17	17.5	18
European	36	37	38	39	41	42	43	44	45

Men – Shoe size conversion

US	7	7.5	8	8.5	9	9.5	10	10.5	11	11.5	12	12.5	13
UK	6	6.5	7	7.5	8	8.5	9	9.5	10	10.5	11	12	12
European	39	40	41	42	43	43	44	44	45	45	46	47	47

My Advice: I think all English men must know of Savile Row, even if they never venture there to see a tailor. You could, however, take your relationship to the next level if you surprise your knight with modern-day armour in the form of an *Ozwald Boateng* bespoke suit!

Shopping — Household Goods

Many of the stores I mentioned in the previous section also carry homeware, and some even sell furniture. You can find specialized retailers, such as bath fitters and kitchen designers, and, whether you have to kit out a flat in Reading or a castle in Coventry, IKEA stores are located throughout England. In most cities or towns, you may find a catalogue store called Argos. We do not have the equivalent of it in the States, but it reminds me of a small warehouse store. When you first walk into the store, there are a few tables with six to eight catalogues on them. You flip through hundreds of pages of household goods. Once you have made your selection, you type the product number into a little blue box in the middle of the table. If the product is available, the quantity will pop-up. You write down the product number and how many of the items you want on an order sheet that is provided at the table. You keep this process going until you have found all the products you need to purchase. You then take your order sheet to the till and pay for your merchandise, and a salesperson goes back to the warehouse to collect your goods and brings them to you. If you prefer not to go into a physical store, you can also purchase items online. If you are not into DIY projects, just as in America, local interior designers can help you create an English home that reflects you.

Driving

In order to obtain a driving licence for a motorcycle or car in England, you need to be seventeen years old or older and pass two parts of the driving skills examination: the knowledge or theory section and the practical section. You must book an appointment time to take both tests. You will be able to take the knowledge component online at one of the closest driving centres to where you live or a location of your choice. You must pass the theory test before you will be allowed to book your practical driving test. Most of the booking and paying of fees can all be done online at the www.gov.uk website under the "Learn to Drive A Car: Step-by-Step" section. You will need to submit a passport-type photo with your licence application.

You can drive on your US licence for up to one year; however, you must register your car with the Driver and Vehicle Licensing Agency (DVLA). In the UK, there is an annual road tax, and if your vehicle is over three years old, it needs an MOT (the common abbreviation for a safety test, pronounced "em-oh-tee") annually. Check the UK government website for specific, updated information.

Learning the traffic signs, road markings and how to navigate your way through a roundabout is not as intuitive as you might think. However, there are three major shapes to the signs, which, if you recognize the shape, even if you don't understand the specifics, you will know its basic function.

Circles – give **commands**

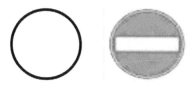

Rectangles- give **information**

Triangles-give **warnings**

You will need to know what "traffic calming" means and what signs such as the one below means:

Traffic calming measures include speed humps and speed cameras. Roundabouts also force drivers to slow down. Parking in England can be a little crazy because it seems everyone needs a space to park but there are limited places. In some residential areas, you will need a permit to park. You will frequently see on-street parking control signs such as this one:

This sign is telling me that parking and loading are restricted, Monday-Saturday from 7:30 – 9:30 in the morning and from 4:30 – 6:30 in the evening. In between these hours, loading and parking are permitted.

In car parks (or as we say in the States, parking lots), you will typically have to pay first for the amount of time your car will spend in the lot. Once you have paid your parking fee, you will receive a date and timed parking ticket to display in your car window. A parking garage is called a "multi-storey". I have to warn you, car park spaces are small and tight, unlike our parking lots in America, in which you have plenty of space to open the car doors and to manoeuvre.

You will need to familiarize yourself with pedestrian, cycle and equestrian signage. Signs for pedestrians are typically directional, are on a bright-blue background with white writing and depict the figure of a person walking in the direction you want to follow.

The signs may vary in colour: brown for a tourist destination;

and green for a public footpath. The signs may also include how far to the destination in yards or miles.

You will need to know the difference between an "A" road and a "B" road, a motorway and a dual-carriage way. The A roads are "major" roads, which are used frequently and are often used to get motorists from point to point. The B roads are more likely to be what in America we call "the back way" roads. They are smaller, maybe more rural or more residential than the A roads, and often have speed restrictions. The motorway is comparable to what in America we call a highway. A dual carriageway is a two-lane highway. I find it especially quaint they reference the days when horse-drawn carriages used these very same roads. For fun, take an educated guess as to what information the next road sign is conveying:

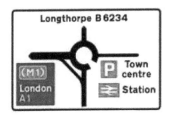

If you recognized the roundabout, well done! This sign gives you a lot of information. The white letter "P" with the blue square background, in the bottom-right corner indicates there is parking in the town centre. There is also a railway station to the right. The "M1" (major motorway) going to London is to the left, and the roundabout can be bypassed with the narrow exit to the left. Longthorpe is straight ahead on road B 6234. You will find a lot of information packed onto many road signs.

On the major motorways, you will find "services" which we call "rest stops". In England, however, the rest stops offer gas, fast food and other travel conveniences. So, they are a lot more comprehensive than our traditional rest stops. The next sign is an example of a services sign.

This sign uses symbols to tell you that services are a half a mile down the road, and you will find bathrooms, fuel, light refreshments and information, but it is not open twenty-four hours a day.

Road markings are also helpful to drivers, cyclists and pedestrians. Take a look at the marking below. This is not a road marking we use in the States.

This yellow box is a marking that you will find at a four-way junction. Your vehicle may not go into the box unless the road is clear where you want to exit. In addition to learning new signs and road markings, you have to keep in mind, even when walking, that everyone drives on the LEFT! Fortunately, in cities that are frequented by tourists, such as London or Bath, there are written road markings that say "Look Left" to remind you to look in the correct direction before stepping out into the road.

My Advice: I failed my driving test the first time! It was the practical side (what we would call the road test) that got me. I was so embarrassed and heartbroken. I had been driving since I was fifteen! What was different? I was driving on the left side of the road; I was driving a manual transmission; there were roundabouts and I was nervous and intimidated. So, I hired a driving instructor. I remember distinctly sitting in my driveway sobbing in Mr Wiggins's car after my first lesson. I thought maybe I should just have Richard drive me around (as he had been doing for months), use public transport or hire a driver, but, being the independent woman that I am, I decided to reframe the picture and keep trying until I succeeded. I finally felt confident in my driving abilities after about the tenth lesson. So, again, I made my way to Trowbridge for my practical exam. As I greeted my examiner, I started to panic. I closed my eyes and took a deep breath and kept telling myself, you can do this, you can do this! Once on the road, I kept praying, please don't tell me to go down a country lane, please, God, no single-track roads. I dreaded driving down some country lanes because many of them were single track, which means that if another car comes from the opposite direction, one driver has to back up until there is a place where the other car can pass. I hated driving in reverse, so, on most occasions, I would just sit and wait until the other car backed up.

As we were driving along, my examiner told me of a recent trip he and his wife had taken to Florida. They had hired (rented) a car and were driving on the Florida turnpike. He really liked the wide roads in, but it was still an anxiety-provoking experience driving in America. The fast lanes on the motorway (highway) are opposite, the signage is slightly different, and he thought turning "right on red" was strange.

So, he felt my pain of learning how-to drive-in England and was quite sympathetic. Needless to say, I passed my practical this time (and there were no country lanes)! I suggest you hire a driving instructor and read all the driving books (*The Highway Code*, the traffic sign book, etc.), which are available on the government website.

Finally, if you are going to hire (rent) a car whilst you are in England and want an automatic, be sure to specify this when making the reservation, otherwise, you will more than likely be given a vehicle with a manual

* All road signs courtesy of Department of Transport, *Know Your Traffic Signs, Official Edition, 2007.*

Health & Wellness

Naturally, you will have to find a doctor, and you can choose either private or free National Health Service (NHS) medical and dental practitioners. This section is not intended to be a tutorial on the NHS. However, I do want to point out a few things to be cognizant of regarding healthcare in England. Depending on where you live, your wait time to see a doctor or book an appointment with the NHS will vary. You also have the option of paying for private healthcare. Your local council's website may have a listing of local hospitals and doctors. Be sure to know that "999" is the number to call for an ambulance, not "911".

Nurses, Dentists and Physicians operate (no pun intended) much the same way as they do in the States, except for a few minor differences in terms. For instance, when you visit the doctor's office, it is referred to as the "doctor's surgery". In the hospital, they use the term "ward" more frequently than we do to differentiate between departments. As an American, when I think of the term "ward", I immediately think of the "psych ward", so it was a little discombobulating when I first went to the hospital in England and heard the term being used over and over again. You may find that some head nurses are called "sister", which I also found strange at first. However, my educated, Catholic-school girl guess is that this term is a carryover from when nurses were also nuns. Specialist doctors are called consultants, so don't be alarmed if your GP wants you to visit a consultant. What we call the emergency room in the States is called the "casualty department", "emergency ward" or "A and E" (accident and emergency) in England. At schools, children may visit matron if they have a cut or fall sick.

Pharmacy — As noted in Chapter 3, the drugstore is called the "chemist's". The most visible chemist's shop in England is Boots. They have locations at Heathrow, Gatwick, the major railway stations and on the high street (main street). Another large chain is Superdrug. Don't forget, band-aids are called "plasters" and they don't sell Tylenol in England.

General Wellness — For overall health and wellness, there are gyms, spas and yoga centres. Everything we have in America for wellness can also be found in England. What is nice about being on the English side of the Atlantic is that you also have the wellness centres of Europe at your doorstep!

Letting or Buying Property

When I lived in London, I rented a one-bedroom apartment on the top floor of a building in Rotherhide. Richard didn't think the neighbourhood was very fashionable, but I loved my flat. It had views of the Thames, and I could catch the ferry, which docked at the hotel next door, to cross over to Canary Wharf, which was on the opposite side of the river. Landlords and estate agents (real estate agents), as they are called in England, advertise rentals as "lettings" or by using the term "to let". Whereas in America, we would say "rent", in England, they say "let".

At some point, you may want to purchase property in England. Until I moved to the UK, I had never heard of the terms "freehold" or "leasehold". A freehold property means you will own the dwelling and the land on which it is built until you decide to sell it. A leasehold means someone else owns the property, and you "lease" it for a period of time. I think of it as renting the property. Leases are for decades; we once looked at a leasehold that was for a hundred years! Leasehold properties are common in England.

My Advice: Whether you decide to rent or buy, be sure you work with a reputable estate agent. Local agents have their pulse on the properties in their area that may be of interest to you. Be sure to read all the documentation and look for rights of way, access, covenants, and any small print. The property could have a public footpath running through it; you don't want to be surprised when someone walks across your front garden. There is also a government tax you must pay when you purchase property or land over a set amount, called a Stamp Duty Land Tax. Educate yourself about the chain process, as a property that is not "chain free" could take a long time to buy. There are also other purchasing schemes, such as shared ownership, that are not offered to home buyers in the U.S.

Utilities & Other Services

This is not an exhaustive list, but if you are moving on your own without the help of a moving coordinator or service, you will want to remember these key points related to setting up house in England.

TV Licence — If you plan to watch television, you need to purchase a licence. I know it seems ridiculous, and I had a hard time wrapping my head around it at first. I thought it was a joke until a note was slipped under my apartment door in London, reminding me to pay my licence fee or be subject to fines.

Electricity — The UK electrical market is privatized, which means you have several companies competing for your business. I have used British Gas and Southern Electric, two of the larger companies, but I would shop around for competitive pricing. The choice of an electricity provider will also partly depend on the area. The UK voltage is 230V. You can use adapters on a short-term basis for small things such as a curling iron or a mobile phone charger, but I suggest purchasing the UK equivalent for long-term use. In England, you will use a three-pin plug, which is known as a "type-G" plug.

The electrical sockets have an "on and off" position. I don't know how many times I have plugged something in and forgotten to turn "on" the socket. Your appliance or whatever you plug in will not work, even if it has a separate power switch, unless the electrical wall outlet is on. These outlets are everywhere except near the bathroom mirror. For some reason, men have a shaving outlet, but women are left to some far-off plug in a different room. This may be changing in newer builds, but good luck finding an outlet to plug in the hair dryer in the bathroom.

Related to the outlets are the light switches. Most light switches in England look like this

and **not** this.

You will also find radiators, even in many of the new builds, which you will sometimes have to bleed or have a handyman do it for you. It's weird—that's all I can say.

I always feel like I'm at my great-grandmother's house when I walk past a radiator, but it is what it is, and if it bothers you too much, they have designer ones and coloured ones. The radiator in my lounge is really tall. I put a monk's bench in front of it, so if you sit there, you are lovely and warm!

The other place you can typically find a heater is in the bathroom for the towels. There is nothing quite like a warm towel when you step out of the bath! An increasingly popular feature in English homes or apartments is underfloor heating. While underfloor heating does exist in the States, I think it is far more common to see it in houses in England. Finally, (although this is not an electrical issue) chances are, your apartment, cottage or house will also come with a fireplace or wood burner for additional heat. The fireplace can be quite cosy on those cold, rainy nights, even if it is gas lit.

Water —Water companies are regionally based, so you will most likely have to sign up for the company that services the area where you live.

Gas — Typically, the same service provider you have for your electricity will also provide your gas.

Parking Permits — Information and applications are available from your local council.

Trash — In England, the trash is called "rubbish", and trash cans are called "rubbish bins". Trash collectors are called "bin men". Trash collection is the responsibility of your local council. It may be a third-party service if you are in a private apartment complex or development.

Recycling is a huge matter in England. You have to separate everything for trash collection, even food waste, which we do not do in most states in America. There is the regular separation of bottles, cans and paper, and then there are separate bins for garden waste. The council can supply you with a little kitchen caddy, or you can compost your food waste. Local recycling centres take the trash that cannot go into your bins. Trash collection varies and may not be weekly in your area. If you are not in the habit of recycling, you might want to start; bin men have rejected trash if it has not been sorted correctly or put in the right bin.

Council Tax — Your council tax pays for the trash pick-up in addition to other community services. How much tax you pay to the council is based on the value of your home. So, it is a good idea to check the council tax band of your home. It could be quite expensive, so you need to make sure you take this into account when budgeting for household expenditures. I recommend looking at your local council's website to learn about the services provided by the council.

Income Tax — Ugh…what else can I say? You have to pay your taxes no matter which country you live in. Essentially, it works in much the same way as taxes in America. You have to pay tax on your income. For most people, their employer will automatically take out the right amount of tax and pay Her Majesty's Revenue & Customs (HMRC) directly. If you are self-employed, you will need to complete a tax return and pay your taxes through the "self-assessment" system. Fortunately, there are help lines and advice available in the HMRC section of the government website: www.gov.uk.

National Insurance — Almost everyone who works in the UK must pay national insurance contributions. It is similar to our social security, as the money from the contributions is used to pay for benefits and state services such as retirement pensions and the NHS. You will need to apply for a National Insurance number. The Department for Work and Pensions (DWP) is responsible for collecting the necessary documentation and distributing the National Insurance numbers. Be sure to contact them either by phone or via the government website listed above.

Pets

My knowledge on this topic is limited since I can only speak to my experience with dogs. Dogs are special to thousands of British households. So, if you are thinking of bringing your furry, four-legged friend with you to the UK, be sure to check the Pets Travel Scheme (PETS) documentation to avoid having your dog endure a six-month quarantine. You must be sure to have your dog micro-chipped and vaccinated. There are also certain "no-fly" times for dogs. Details can be found by calling the airline you are flying. It is worth checking the requirements for restrictions well in advance of your move.

It is worth noting that you MUST clean up after your dog. There are dog-waste containers in most parks. Some places even offer disposable plastic waste bags in case you forgot to bring yours or have run out. Most of the time, your dog must be on a lead (leash). I was fortunate to have a dog-walking service supplement my dog walking. These services can be quite useful if you are unable to exercise the dog (which was my case) as frequently as needed.

> **My Advice:** Have an international pet transportation specialist service make the travel arrangements for your four-legged friend. Also, be prepared to pay top dollar for your pet to fly from the States to England. The airline ticket for my dog to fly from Nashville to London was twice as much as mine! I am talking thousands of dollars I had to pay for Moo-Moo to relocate.

I know I have left out many things, but hopefully, this chapter contains enough information to help get you underway. The first time I moved to England, it took me a year to settle, even with Richard's help. The acclimatization period varies for everyone. Don't rush the process and don't give up, especially if you're in love.

CHAPTER 8

Happily, Ever After

Well, there you have it, my guidance and advice on how to better understand your Englishman. Of course, all men are different, but now you have some insight from an American woman who has first-hand experience of dating and marrying an Englishman. The trajectory of my life changed at Los Angeles International Airport the day Richard said to me, "You are my future", as he boarded a plane for London Heathrow. He was right! I was his future, and he was mine. I left Venice, California, for Frome, England, and after a tumultuous two years in England, I finally settled. Richard proposed at the Lawrence Hill bus depot car park in Bristol.

My first engagement ring looked like something out of a Cracker Jack box. It was temporary, as Richard said he envisioned buying a loose diamond and having it fitted into a setting of my choice. He told me looking for the right engagement ring was going to be an adventure. He arranged for us to travel to Brussels first. We had a lovely weekend searching for a ring, but to no avail. Richard then planned a trip to New York City. We were confident that we could find a diamond there. Plus, the pound to the dollar was quite high and jewellers in Manhattan were going to be competitive with their Hatton Garden counterparts in London. We only had a few days in the city therefore, we had arranged for a few jewellers to meet us at our hotel. We were staying at a hotel called *The Mark*, close to where my friend from Vassar, Jean, was living, just off Madison Avenue. She met us for drinks at the hotel bar to discuss our trip to the diamond district the next day. Jean had played an important role in the beginning of my relationship with Richard because when I was contemplating a trip to England to see him, she was visiting me in Los Angeles. I'll never forget she was staying at *Shutters* in Santa Monica and we were talking on the veranda overlooking the Pacific Ocean. I was wavering and told her I couldn't really afford the expense of flying to London. Jean convinced me I should go. She was so strong in her conviction that she bought the airline ticket for me. In many ways, she started me on my romantic journey, which is why she was the maid of honour at my wedding.

After Brussels, Richard and I were armed with much more information and better prepared to buy a quality diamond. I thought I wanted a princess-cut diamond set in platinum. We had done our homework and were more concerned with colour and clarity than with size. Our adventure in the diamond district took us from shop to shop, from one side of the street to the other, up and down the block, until finally, we found it. By the time I had settled on an engagement ring, I had changed my mind from a princess cut to an emerald cut. We had spent the entire day in the district following my diamond around from the shop, to the setter, to the polisher and then, back to the shop. We followed the shop girl through underground passages and vaults full of jewels. I had never seen anything like it. The diamond never left our sight. In the end, Richard had his GIA certificate, and I had my custom-designed engagement ring. I didn't end up with a princess-cut diamond, but I sure did feel like a princess that weekend! It was a truly once-in-a-lifetime shopping experience. The next day, as we were leaving the hotel to explore Manhattan, we saw the news presenter Christiane Amanpour waiting in the lobby. Apparently, she was there to interview the then Venezuelan president, who was also staying at The Mark. We were visiting the city at the same time there was a meeting at the United Nations. Tony Blair was prime minister and staying at a hotel across Madison Avenue. We could see his secret service detail from our hotel window. It was all very exciting for this Motor City girl! I look at this same beautiful ring on my finger today, and it always brings back the best memories of that trip to New York.

I was thirty-eight years old when I married. We were married in England. Our marriage certificate referred to me as "Spinster". I can look back and laugh at the terminology now, but when I first saw it, I was aghast. I thought of a spinster as a little old lady with cats overrunning her house! I also had to be interviewed at the registry office to ensure I was not being forced into the marriage. Throughout the interview, I kept thinking to myself, I'm thirty-eight years old, who would be forcing me, a grown woman, into marriage? I suppose the Wiltshire registry office wanted to be safe rather than sorry and was only following protocol. The planning for and build-up to my wedding day was truly an experience. I could write another book for Americans on how to plan a wedding in England.

My big day finally arrived, and so did a little bit of rain, but it was one of the happiest days of my life. My parents and my college friends from Vassar, Maxine, Jean and Lisa, all attended. My sister, Avila, Maxine and Jean were all bridesmaids. They wore simple, dusty-rose-pink Laura Ashley dresses I'd bought off the sale rack at the store in Bath. The colour of their dresses was a beautiful complement to my blush-pink wedding gown. My dress had been designed by a wedding dressmaker in Newport Pagnell, who specialized in petite women's designs. It was made of thick silk, lace and a little tulle underneath. Although it was a light shade of pink, it looked more cream in the pictures.

Lisa's twins, Alexandra and Jacques, were the flower girl and ring bearer, respectively. Lisa wrapped Alex's arm in pink silk ribbon to cover the cast on her broken arm. She also picked flowers from our garden to make a small posy for Alex to carry. The day before the wedding, she spent creating and printing the order of service. My mom, dad, sister and niece Loren all sat around the dining room table putting the finishing touches on the wedding favours.

I'll never forget the days leading up to my wedding. I was surrounded by the people who loved me the most in the world. I was fortunate that Richard's daughters, Joanne and Zoe, accepted and treated me well. I didn't have a "hen do"; the closest I came to celebrating with just the girls was a few days before the wedding, going to the Pump Room for lunch and then to the milliner's in Bath and choosing the hats they would wear for the wedding. Richard and the groomsmen (except for Joanne) wore traditional morning suits and top hats. They were barely able to rent top hats as the wedding was the same weekend as Ascot, and top hats were being rented out continuously. Richard had asked his eldest daughter to be his "best (wo)man", which I thought was a lovely gesture. My sister's husband, Charlie, and Richard's good mate Steve rounded out the wedding party. It was a small wedding, with only about fifty guests. My immediate family and close American friends who were able to fly over to England attended. Kevin, a friend of Richard's, who is a classic bus enthusiast, agreed to let us hire his classic Bristol LHT half-cab bus to transport the American guests to and from the wedding. The driver had a ticket with our wedding date stamped on it for each guest who boarded the bus. We used the same vehicle ten years later at our anniversary celebration. Can you spot the error in the picture?

Our wedding was held at *Lucknam Park Hotel* in Colerne, Wiltshire, near Chippenham (https://www.lucknampark. co.uk/), and it will always hold a special place in my heart for its classic English elegance and beauty. My parents were celebrating their forty-ninth wedding anniversary the day before my wedding, so we decided to have a celebratory anniversary dinner at the hotel and spend the night. The then hotel manager, Harry, arranged for my parents to have one of the grand suites in the main house. It was so beautiful; the wedding photographer took pictures in the room. My room was down the hall, and it too was lovely. Maxine came to stay with me and calmed my prewedding jitters. Upon our arrival, we took tea in the room and enjoyed the view of the grounds and long driveway. Maxine, the classical pianist, somehow found out that Pavarotti had stayed in the very same room on a visit to the area, and she delighted in telling me this fact.

On June 26, 2004, I remember my dad taking my hand as we were about to walk down the aisle and begin the wedding ceremony, asking, "Are you ready, Chief?" I had smiled and nodded my head. At that moment, the photographer called to us, and we both looked back. That was the last time I entered a room as a single woman.

The wedding ceremony went off without a hitch. We had come full circle, my Englishman and I, from that first date in Santa Monica when we'd heard Jimi Hendrix playing in the background, to the West Country of England, when we concluded our marriage ceremony by processing out of the room to Jimi Hendrix's "Little Wing" being played by a young classical guitarist.

The wedding breakfast was perfection. Canapés and champagne were served in the library and main reception room as guests waited for pictures to be taken and the wedding breakfast to begin. The flowers, food and cake were all locally sourced from the West Country. We had requested buttercream frosting and real flowers be placed on the cake. I danced for the first time as a married woman, to "At Last" by Etta James. It seemed a fitting song, seeing how my spinster days were behind me and *at last*, I had managed to find a suitable mate. It was a glorious day that was over too quickly. We left the next day for our honeymoon in Anguilla, where we were able to completely relax at our *Covecastles* villa and then spend our final days at the *Malliouhana* hotel.

The choice to have a ceilidh band and dancing for the reception was to be repeated at our tenth wedding anniversary celebration. We held our tenth anniversary party in conjunction with our son's baptism. Everything took place in the lovely Somerset village of Mells. The christening was at St. Dominic's Catholic Chapel, which is set in the grounds of the manor house at Mells. Remember, I mentioned an error in the picture of the old Bristol bus? The bus destination reads "Wells", not "Mells".

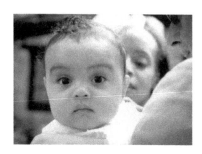

The anniversary/christening meal was served family-style at the *Talbot Inn* (https://www.talbotinn.com/), and I wore my wedding dress (although I had it shortened to tea length) for ceilidh dancing at the Mells Tithe Barn. Once again, just as we had been at our wedding we were surrounded by both English and American family and friends.

The Family: Frederica, Jackson, Richard, Joanne & Zoe at Jackson's Christening in Mells.

As I sit in my "Rosie the Riveter" t-shirt, writing this final section of the book, I thank God for the many blessings I have received, including one of the most important, my husband. I am the modern American woman. However, I did not get to this place alone. I am grateful to the amazing women both American and English (Comfort, Jan, Elaine, Celena and Monica) who have helped me live my dream. I also know that without my best friend and the love of my life, Richard, I would not be the wife, mother, sister, aunt, friend, psychologist, or citizen that I am.

"Happily, ever after" only happens in fairy tales. In real life, relationships, and marriage in particular, take hard work and compromise. There are ups and downs, and some days, I wonder if I am living on a different planet from my husband. There are days when I know that what I am saying is going in one of Richard's ears and out the other. Every year, when I am filling out our tax organizer, I wonder if I made the right decision, marrying a foreigner and living in a different country. Since we split our time between both countries, we have to file our taxes in both countries. (I am eternally grateful to Bruce Jaffe, the international tax consultant who first took me on as an utterly confused tax client.) Who knew love could be this complex on so many levels? I certainly didn't. Knowing what I know now, would I marry him all over again? Yes, emphatically, yes! Richard is my companion through my life's journey (literally and figuratively). I would not have seen temples in Bangkok, the Rock of Gibraltar or visited Morocco without him. Together, we have explored Route 66 and sailed into New York on the Queen Mary 2. Plus, there is no one who can make my cup of tea like Richard!

So, it is with good intent that I have written this book for the American woman who is considering dating or marrying an Englishman. I have written the book as a practical (and humorous) guide to having a successful relationship with an Englishman. I am a Black, middle-class, working woman, originally from Detroit. I never thought growing up that I would marry a foreigner and live the life of a dual citizen. Occasionally, when I meet a new sorority sister (Alpha Kappa Alpha, Incorporated), she'll ask if my husband is Greek. I smile and say, "no, he's English". My husband comes from a working-class, Bristolian family. He can put on the BBC British accent or the Tennessee southern drawl with ease. We flow and flourish in both countries. Most importantly, we are regular, everyday people. He's not royalty, and I am not an American heiress. We are two people with shared interests, values and love for each other. We also appreciate and respect each other's country and rich cultural heritage. We talk about the painful parts of our history. For Richard, it is the history of colonization and the British involvement in the Trans-Atlantic slave trade. Richard is keenly aware of Bristol's (and Liverpool's) involvement and investment in the commoditization of human beings. For me, it was visiting my grandmother in the segregationist south and seeing Klansmen in full robes. It was the derogatory name-calling and the unwillingness of others to see beyond the colour of my skin that was extremely hurtful. Fortunately, we are living in the 21ˢᵗ century and we hope society will be a better place for our son. We will teach him not to forget whence he came and to embrace his mixed-race heritage, for it is special and unique.

I have written this book from the perspective of a modern American woman. I generalize and make interpretations about the English from my own unique vantage point. So, take and use those tips and advice that you have found useful and ignore what you have not. I hope that you will find your Prince Charming and live your life the closest to "happily ever after" that you can.

Photo Credits and Picture Attributions (in order of appearance)

Chapter 1

Map of the United Kingdom:
By Source:File:British Isles all.svg by CnbrbFile:United Kingdom countries.svg by Rob984Derived work:Offnfopt - United Kingdom countries.svg, CC BY-SA 4.0, https://commons.wikimedia.org/w/index.php?curid=39213409

Map of England with counties and transport routes:
User:(WT-shared) Burmesedays, SVG of the UK at Commons, Perry-Castañeda Library Map Collection UK Maps, OpenStreetMap, User:(WT-shared) Paul. / CC BY-SA (https://creativecommons.org/licenses/by-sa/3.0)

Roman Baths, Bath Spa:
By Diego Delso, CC BY-SA 4.0, https://commons.wikimedia.org/w/index.php?curid=35323216

White Rose, House of York:
https://commons.wikimedia.org/wiki/File:Yorkshire_rose.png

Red Rose, House of Tudor:
https://commons.wikimedia.org/wiki/File:Lancashire_rose.svg

Bushmills, photo credit: Wagrati Photo.

Chapter 2

Map of England with counties and transport routes: User:(WT-shared) Burmesedays, SVG of the UK at Commons, Perry-Castañeda Library Map Collection UK Maps, OpenStreetMap, User:(WT-shared) Paul. / CC BY-SA (https://creativecommons.org/licenses/by-sa/3.0)

Chapter 3

Physical Map of United Kingdom, mapswire: https://mapswire. com/countries/united-kingdom/CC BY-SA 4.0

Chapter 4

Zoe and I at Breakfast, Personal Photograph Collection.

Richard in the Kitchen, Personal Photograph Collection.

Chapter 5

Ettle Family, Personal Photograph Collection.

Ballons over Bristol, *photo credit: Angharad Paull.*

Chapter 7

Radiator Image by Gelly at Pixabay.

All road signs courtesy of Department of Transport, *Know Your Traffic Signs, Official Edition, 2007*. Images are Crown copyright.

Moo-Moo the dog, Personal Photograph Collection.

Chapter 8

All pictures from Personal Photograph Collection.

Photographs not listed are either in the public domain or listed under the Creative Commons license and do not require attribution for use.